W9-BTT-272

The Book of Forms

LEWIS TURCO, born in Buffalo, New York, in 1934, is Associate Professor of English at the State University College, Oswego, New York. He received his B.A. at the University of Connecticut in 1959 and his M.A. from the University of Iowa in 1962. He has held poetry fellowships at Yaddo, Bread Loaf, and at the Writers' Workshop of the University of Iowa. Mr Turco is the author of three books of poetry: *First Poems* (1960), *The Sketches* (1962), and *Awaken, Bells Falling* (1968). He was the founder, and for three years director, of the Cleveland State University Poetry Center. In addition, Mr. Turco has contributed prose and poetry to many journals, including *The Atlantic Monthly*, *The New Yorker*, *Poetry* (Chicago), *Saturday Review*, *American Scholar*, *Kenyon Review*, *Paris Review*, and *Sewanee Review*. His poem "November 22, 1963" has been widely reprinted in this country and translated abroad, and it serves as the basis for a ballet "While the Spider Slept," performed by the Royal Swedish Ballet.

The Book of Forms

A Handbook of Poetics

LEWIS TURCO

New York   E. P. Dutton & Co., Inc.   1968

For Vern and Mort and,
in some ways, better days.

Contents

Introduction

The Book of Forms: A Handbook of Poetics is intended as a text and reference work for students of poetry in general, and of verse composition in particular. Although the accent is on the forms of poetry, this volume contains all the information essential to the student of contemporary poetics.

In addition, *The Book of Forms* has a number of unique and unusual features:

I. "Some Notes on Metrics" is a chapter that surveys the various prosodic and metrical systems, clarifies such terms as *rhythm*, *cadence*, and *meter*, and provides clear explanations of the processes and methods of versification. At the end of the chapter there is a table that lists the symbols used in the schematic diagrams of the various verse forms set forth in Chapter Four.

II. The chapter entitled "Some Notes on Sonics" begins with a concise definition of the poem as a series of levels—"visible," "sonic," "sensory," and "ideational"—that, taken together, form a "fusional level" of interrelationships. From this point, the chapter proceeds to a discussion of the techniques of the sonic devices of poetry—such as rhyme, elision, alliteration, etc.—that were not covered in the first chapter.

III. The concern of Chapter Three, "Some Notes on Tropes," is with figurative language and the various aspects of what was once called "wit" and, more recently, the faculty of "fancy"—allusions, symbolism, metaphor, irony, and so forth. The chapter concludes with a discussion of the various kinds of "ambiguity" in poetry.

IV. Chapter Four is the heart of the volume. It is really a book-within a-book; therefore, it is titled, "The Book of Forms." It is divided into three parts:

1) The first part of this chapter is a "Form–Finder," in which all the forms contained in the volume are listed and divided, first into *regular* poem and stanza forms, and then into *irregular* forms. Under *regular forms* there are further subdivisions, beginning with *one-line forms* and working through *two-hundred-ten-line forms*.

Should a student wish to know the form of a poem he has been studying, rather than leaf through all the forms in the book, he may first determine a) the *rhyme scheme* of the poem or stanza in question and b) its *meter*. Then he may c) *count the lines of his form* and turn to the Form-Finder. There, under the appropriate heading, he will find a short list of stanza and poem patterns, which he may investigate in order to determine the exact name of the form he wishes to identify.

Similarly, should a student of verse composition wish to attempt a form of a specific length, he may use the Form-Finder to discover an interesting structure. Many students find that there is no quicker way to improve as writers than through formal experimentation and attempts to solve specific technical problems.

2) The second section of Chapter Four is intended to be the most comprehensive rehearsal of the verse forms that are *traditional in Anglo-American prosody:* over 175 specific forms are listed alphabetically.

Our heritage of forms is very rich. We are heirs not only of British metric systems, but also of systems derived from Europe, the Middle East, and Asia. Our history of verse forms goes back through the Normans, the Anglo-Saxons, and the Celts, and we have derived much from the systems of the Hebrews, the Greeks, the Italians, and the French.

The verse forms here set forth have all been utilized at one time or another by poets of the British Isles and North America. During four periods of the history of English letters, particularly, poets have used and extended the forms here described. During the Middle Ages, the Renaissance, the Romantic, and the Victorian periods, and throughout the twentieth century—but particularly the contemporary era—there have been craftsmen who have explored the possibilities of the formal structure of verse.

True as this is, to this point no attempt has been made at a systematic survey of our traditional forms *in toto*, and to make them all available, in as clear a manner as possible, to students, student-poets, and the poets themselves.

Chapter Four is just such an attempt, and it contains a number of features that no other volume at present offers:

A) A *unique* schematic diagramming system for all forms. By studying the diagrams one can see readily the structures of the various forms.

B) *Concise* prose descriptions of the forms.

C) *Complete* cross-references, so that students can discover relationships and similarities among many of the forms.

An additional word ought to be said on this last subject: while researching these forms, the author has discovered ambiguities in many of the descriptions set forth by his sources. He has also found that in several cases distinctly different forms have been lumped under one terminology or another. In order to clarify the study of verse forms, in some cases the author has invented the names of forms, but in every case these inventions are *derived from the original ambiguous terminology*. In no instance has a form itself been invented. On the other hand, a number of the classical forms have not been used in English poetry, and these have been excluded from consideration, as have some invented forms— such as the Clerihew or the many varieties of sonnets other than the major forms. However, invented forms, like the Keatsian ode, that have passed into the body of our tradition are fully covered. Some forms, such as the line invented by Ogden Nash or the contemporary eighteen-line accentual poem—pioneered by William Carlos Williams and adopted by the younger poets—set forth on page 130, have not formerly had names at all, and nomenclature has been supplied as logic might dictate.

3) The third and last section of Chapter Four is a bibliog-

raphy of *contemporary* poems written in traditional forms. This bibliography has been included so that students may see, if they wish, how poets of today have adapted forms to our modern idiom and needs.

V. *The Book of Forms: A Handbook of Poetics* concludes with a "Glossarial Index" containing over 650 entries, of which there are three kinds:

1) Entries of technical terms, with page numbers, that appear in the various chapters and in the Introduction, with cross-references.

2) Entries for synonyms of terms found in *1)* above, with cross-references.

3) Definitions of various terms not covered elsewhere in the volume, with cross-references.

It will be seen, then, that the Glossarial Index is in itself a fifth chapter—a handbook in small—and it should be utilized as such.

LEWIS TURCO

Oswego, New York

Acknowledgments and Bibliography of Sources

The author wishes to express his thanks to Dr. Donald Justice, formerly Assistant Director of the Writers' Workshop of the State University of Iowa and now Professor of English at Syracuse University, for his early encouragement and advice; to Dr. Donald R. Tuttle of the Office of Education, U.S. Department of Health, Education, and Welfare for his critical suggestions and revisions; to Professor John Montague of the University of California, Berkeley, for remarks concerning the Irish forms; to Professor Philip Legler of Sweet Briar College for his encouragement in print; to Messrs. Fred Cogswell of the University of New Brunswick, Canada, and Alexander Craig of Victoria, Australia, for their early cooperation; to Professor William Keen of State University College, Oswego, New York, for suggesting the form-finder; to Professor Arnold G. Tew of Cleveland State University, whose help with the irregular forms was invaluable; to Mr. Dudley Fitts of Phillips Andover, Paul Engle of Iowa, Richard Eberhart of Dartmouth, John Ciardi of Bread loaf, and the many other poets and friends who have, at one stage or another, provided encouragement during the seven-year odyssey of this manuscript.

The author is particularly indebted to the various librarians associated with the White Collection of Medieval Literature of the Cleveland Public Library. They were of incalculable aid, as were these books:

Bridges, Robert, *Milton's Prosody*, Oxford: Oxford University Press, 1893.

Cohen, Helen Louise, *Lyric Forms from France*, New York: Harcourt, Brace and Co., 1922.

Davison, Edward Lewis, *Some Modern Poets, and Other Essays*, New York: Harper and Brothers, 1928.

Humpries, Rolfe, *Green Armor on Green Ground*, New York: Charles Scribner's Sons, 1956.

Justice, Donald, *Of Prosody: Notes for a Course in Contemporary Poetry*, Iowa City: privately circulated, 1959.

Knott, Eleanor, *Irish Classical Poetry*, Dublin: Colm O Lochlainn at the Sign of the Three Candles, 1960.

———*Irish Syllabic Poetry* 1200–1600, Dublin and Cork: Cork University Press, 1935.

Preminger, Alex, *Encyclopedia of Poetry and Poetics*, Princeton: Princeton University Press, 1965.

Untermeyer, Louis, *The Forms of Poetry*, New York: Harcourt, Brace and Co., 1926.

Williams, Gwyn, *An Introduction to Welsh Poetry*, London: Faber and Faber, 1953.

Wood, Clement, *Poets' Handbook*, New York: Greenberg, 1940.

Wrinn, Mary J.J., *The Hollow Reed*, New York: Harper and Brothers, 1935.

Chapter One
Some Notes on Metrics

Before one can begin to study the craft of verse construction systematically, one must understand something about rhythm, for rhythm is at the root of traditional English poetry. One of the basic functions of the poet is the *ordering of the rhythms of language*.

Three words must be defined before we can proceed further. The first is the word *rhythm* itself, and it may be defined as "The flow of cadences in written or spoken language."*

In order to go on to the job of ordering the rhythms of language, the poet must know the definitions of two other words: *prosody* and *meter*. Prosody may be defined as "The science or art of versification; specifically (a) The systematic study of metrical structure, including varieties of poetic feet and meters, rhymes and rhyming patterns, types of stanzas and strophes, and fixed forms. (b) A particular system or theory of versification or of metrical compositions; as Horace's *prosody*.

"The principal symbols for representing features of prosody are: ´ ictus or accent; · secondary accent; | a division between feet. Thus, My lóve | is líke | a rèd, | red róse. In quantitative verse: ᴜ– is for an iamb; –ᴜ a trochee; –ᴜᴜ a dactyl; ᴜᴜ– an anapest; ––a spondee." Three other metrical units which sometimes occur are ᴜᴜ the pyrrhic; ᴜ–ᴜ the amphibrach, and ᴜᴜᴜ the tribrach, and –ᴜ– the amphimacer. The symbols used in scansion are ᴜ the *breve* and – the macron. The virgule / is a stroke that is used to indicate a division between *verses,* not verse feet.

*Since one of the dictionaries most commonly used by students is the *Webster's New Collegiate Dictionary*, all the quoted definitions of words used in this section are taken from the 2nd edition (1951) of the *New Collegiate* published by the G. & C. Merriam Co., Publishers, Springfield, Massachusetts.

For the purposes of this book, the differences between the *primary accent* (ictus) and the secondary accent will be ignored. Instead, reliance will be placed upon a system that distinguishes only between the accented (–) syllable and the unaccented (υ) syllable. Thus, an iamb (υ–) consists of one *verse foot* containing two syllables: the first syllable is un-accented; the second syllable is accented. A dactyl (–υυ) consists of a verse foot having three syllables, the first syllable being accented, the second and third syllables unaccented. We shall have more to say on this subject later.

To return to our definitions, *meter* may be thus defined: "Systematically arranged and measured rhythm in verse; specifically (a) The property of a verse that is divided into feet or syllabic groups. (b) The pattern of a verse marked by the prevailing foot and the number of feet."

To recapitulate main points, then:

1. *Rhythm* is *the flow of cadences in written or spoken languages.*
2. *Prosody* is *the science or art of versification.*
3. *Meter* is *the pattern of a verse.*

There are traditionally in English prosody four kinds of meters. Each kind has been called by other names, but for clarity we shall refer to them as *accentual, syllabic, accent-tual-syllabic,* and *free verse*. Strictly speaking, the last "meter," free verse, is not *metrical* (measured), for its nature is denoted by its name: the rhythms are *free* or *unpatterned*. For this reason it has been said that free verse is the most difficult of the prosodic bases, for the free-verse poet must have developed an ear for rhythms in order to keep from slipping from verse into prose. For further discussion of free verse and prose rhythms, see the section on FREE VERSE in Chapter Four.

Before discussing the other three meters, we must over-come one other word: *scansion*, and again we resort to the dictionary. To *scan* means "To go through (verse) foot by foot distinguishing the metrical structure."

Any kind of language, even prose, may be scanned. Thus, if you will note the marks above this phrase, you will see that it has been scanned into a series of five iambs, or iambic feet. Each syllable is either accented or unaccented in *normal* speech. Five iambic feet is a measure frequently found in English verse. It is called *iambic pentameter*, which brings up another semantic problem. Simply, *penta-* (from the Greek *pente*) means *five*. Thus, *iambic pentameter* means *a measure of five iambic feet*. Similarly, *mono-* means *one*; *di-* means *two*; *tri-* means *three*; *tetra-* means four; *hexa-* means *six*, and so forth.

Any of these prefixes linked to the word *meter* will denote a certain number of verse feet in a line of verse. By scanning the line it is usually possible to distinguish the *predominating* kind of verse foot in the line. Thus, *anapestic trimeter* means a line·of verse in which there are three anapests, *or* in which there are *at least two* anapests, plus one other kind of verse foot.

It is important to note the last point: that scansion attempts only to establish the *normative meter*, for no true poet writes always in regular measures. When a person scans a poem and decides that the poem is written in iambic tetrameter, he is only describing a norm. Some lines may not contain even one iamb, but most lines will; moreover, in most lines iambs will *predominate*.

May we return for a moment to our definition of meter? Meter is "the pattern of a verse." It is only that—a pattern. One feature which distinguishes a poet from a versifier is that a poet *understands a pattern and works against it*, while a versifier *memorizes a pattern and works with it*.

There is nothing more monotonous than a regular beat carried over an extended period of time. Think of the metronome. But *counterpoint* (or syncopation)—rhythmical variation against a regular beat—contains the element of surprise, and handled skilfully, it can be most pleasing. When a poet establishes a metrical norm in his verses he sets into motion in the mind of the reader a regular cadence against which the poet will impose a series of rhythmical variations. If handled well, these variations will not seem dissonant (except for deliberately designed effects), but musically pleasing.

Such skill, however, is usually acquired only after much practice, study, and work: there is as much craft and understanding of technique required in the art of poetry as in any of the other arts. It takes patience as well as inspiration to be a bard, or *maker*, as the poet was originally called.

But we were discussing meters. The first of the three prosodic systems with which we have to deal is *accentual verse*. In accentual verse the only important metrical consideration is the number of *accented syllables* to the line. There may be any number of unaccented syllables in any given line of verse. For examples of accentual verse, see the sections on ANGLO-SAXON PROSODY, the PEARLINE STANZA, and the TRIVERSEN.

The second of the prosodic systems is *syllabic verse*. Here, the only important metrical consideration is the number of *syllables* to the line. There may be any number of stresses or accents in any given line. For examples of syllabic verse see the Welsh and Irish forms, the French forms, and the HAIKU, TANKA, and CINQUAIN.

The third system, *accentual-syllabic verse*, is the usual prosodic standard of English poetry. It depends for its basic pattern upon the more-or-less *regular alternation* of *stressed* and *unstressed* syllables.

Once again, it should be noted that these descriptions are descriptions of norms only, of patterns. For instance, in accentual-syllabic verse a perfect line of iambic pentameter will consist of ten syllables: five unaccented and five accented syllables alternated regularly beginning with an unaccented syllable. But the poet may vary this basic pattern in a number of ways: by substituting one kind of verse foot for another; by means of enjambment, caesura, and elision; by varying the quality and quantity of syllables. But these points will be taken up in the next chapter.

Some explanation must be given of the system of metrical notation which has been developed for *The Book of Forms*. The schematic diagrams that appear beneath most of the prose explications of these various forms, lines, and stanza patterns are designed to present visually 1) the number of syllables to the line of verse; 2) the number of accents to the line; 3) the rhyme schemes, and 4) the positions of rhymed and unrhymed refrains and repetitions. For these reasons, the traditional method of scansion is not used. Hence, the following symbols should be noted:

(x)	—Small *x* stands for an unrhymed syllable that is either unaccented or whose accent is unimportant;
(′)	—A slant stands for an accent (stress);
(x́)	—Stands for an unrhymed, *accented* syllable.
(a, b, c . . .)	—Small letters *other than x* stand for rhymes.
(á, b́, ć . . .)	—Small accented letters *other than x* stand for stressed rhymed syllables.
(A, B, C . . .)	—1. In the Welsh and Irish forms, capital letters stand for *main* rhymes.
	—2. In the French forms, capital letters (except *R*) indicate *rhymed refrains that are whole lines* or *repetons:* whole lines that are repeated, but that are *not* refrains.
(R)	—In some French forms, *R* indicates a *refrain that consists of only a part of a line.*
(A¹, B¹, A², B²)	—Numbered capital letters indicate *sequence of refrains.*
(or)	—In certain Welsh forms *or* indicates a syllable or word that *off-rhymes.*
(oe, ay, ei . . .)	—1. In certain Welsh forms, grouped letters (other than *x*'s and *or*) indicate *diphthong rhymes.*
(c, xc, bc)	—2. In certain Irish forms, a small *c* used alone or grouped with other letters, indicates *consonance*, not rhyme.
(xxx, xax, xxb)	—3. Otherwise, grouped letters indicate a *word* consisting of so many syllables.
(*x x a* x x)	—In the Welsh and Irish forms, *italicized* syllables indicate *possible positions* for

rhymes, cross-rhymes, assonances, or alliterations.

(·)   —A dot stands for a *caesura* (or pause) in the center of a line.

If these symbols seem confusing out of context, they will become immediately clear once you turn to the schematic diagrams themselves.

There will be certain exceptions to these rules, but in each case the exceptions will be apparent and will be stated in the heading for each diagram.

Chapter Two
Some Notes on Sonics

A poem is a series of language patterns. The first and least important pattern is on the *visible level:* how does the poem look on paper? This is not irrelevant, for if one will compare how a poem by Walt Whitman looks in print, with the aspect of a poem by, perhaps, William Carlos Williams, one can tell the difference at a glance, perhaps even catch some impression of the unlike psychological effects these poems will produce on close reading. There is even one form, SPATIALS or *hieroglyphic verse*, that depends for its rationale on how the poem is set up in type.

Second, there is the *sonic level*, a much more important consideration: what musical or sonoral sequence does the poet weave?

Third, there is the *sensory level:* what mood does the poet evoke? What emotions, scenes, desires, and so forth.

Fourth, there is the *ideational level:* meaning, theme, philosophy, observation, moral.

Fifth, there is the *fusional level:* what does the combination of ingredients equal?

In this chapter we will deal with aspects of the sonic level that were not covered in the preceding chapter on metrics.

It has been pointed out that a regular rhythm repeated endlessly is monotonous. Since rhythm is a basic sonic effect, the poet must know something about how to vary his meters.

The primary analyzable methods of metrical variation lie in *quality, quantity, caesura, enjambment*, and *elision*.

QUALITY has to do with the substitution of one kind of verse foot for another, specifically of a verse foot different from the measure of the norm that has been established in the poem.

QUANTITY has to do with variation in the "length" of a syllable. The norm of a line of verse frequently establishes that the *long syllable sound* coincides with the *accented syllable*.

The substitution of a *short* or normally unaccented syllable for a long, normally accented syllable, and vice versa, constitutes a subtle method of rhythmic variation.

CAESURA is a rhythmic pause in the center of a line. The pause may be created by the manipulation of measures, by phrasing, or by punctuation.

ENJAMBMENT has to do with run-on lines. The normal expectation is that phrasing will be completed at the end of a line of verse or other metrical unit, such as a couplet or stanza, and that a pause or *end-stop* will ensue. Enjambment occurs when there is no pause at the end of the line and the phrase carries over into the next line.

ELISION has to do with the melding of two or more sounds into a single syllable or syllable sound. Bridges* has codified some of the analyzable methods of eliding:

1. *Vowels:* "When two vowel sounds come together, then if the first of the two has a tail-glide (a y-glide or a w-glide), there may be elision."

   a. Examples of y-glide:* come *flying; be it* so; *the oth*er men; *thee and* she; glory *a*bove; *riot.*

   b. Examples of *w*-glide: *ruin*ous; *so oft*en; al*so in*; Maro*cco, or* Trebisond; fol*lowers;* sha*dowy;* gra*dual;* in*fluence.*

2. "*H* is often considered as no letter." Examples: ought *to have; to her*self; on*ly who.*

3. *Semi-vowels:* "If two unstressed vowels be separated by *r* there may be elision." Donald Justice† adds: "This applies also to *l* and *n* and perhaps may be extended to *m*." Examples:

   mur*muring;* pil*lar of* State; invisi*ble else;* rea*son has;* i*ron ore;* bego*tten, and.*

Further, according to Justice, "Final *m* and *n* are very frequently not counted anyhow, as in *chasm* or *heaven.* The words *evil* and *spirit* have also been frequently taken in English verse to have but one syllable. In contrast, *fire*

Milton's Prosody by Robert Bridges, Oxford: Oxford University Press, 1893.

†Examples and quotations taken from *Of Prosody* by Donald Justice, Iowa City, Iowa, 1960.

often is counted as two, *e.g.* Other characteristic words illustrating semi-vowel elision: suf*f*ering, endea*v*oring, gen*e*ral, se*v*eral, des*p*erate, am*o*rous, con*qu*eror, po*p*ular, gro*v*eling, bu*s*iness, har*d*ening, lum*in*ous, o*p*ening.

"Elision in most of these words is optional; that is, the word need not be elided each time it occurs, even if it occurs twice in the same line."

MISCELLANEOUS DEVICES for rhythmic variation:

1. A perfect metrical line of verse is called an *acatalectic* line; the noun is *acatalexis*.

   a. By *dropping* a syllable at the *end* of the line, the line is made *catalectic;* the noun is *catalexis*.

   b. By *adding* a syllable at the *end* of the line, the line is made *hypercatalectic;* the noun is *hypercatalexis*.

   c. By *dropping* unaccented syllables from the *beginning* of the line, the line is made *acephalous;* the noun is *acephalexis*.

   d. By *adding* unaccented syllables to the *beginning* of the line, the line is made *anacrustic;* the noun is *anacrusis*.

The similarity and dissimilarity of sounds also are important to the poet:

TRUE RHYME consists of the *identical* sounds, in two or more words, of an *accented vowel* together with *all sounds following* that vowel while the *consonantal* sounds immediately *preceding* the vowel *differ* in each word. Thus, *b*ite, *tr*ite, *sl*eight, *n*ight, and de*l*ight are true rhymes.

FALSE RHYME has to do with the *identical* sound of the *consonant* or consonants immediately *preceding* the accented vowel, plus the vowels' subsequent sounds in two or more words. Thus, *c*yst, in*s*ist, per*s*ist, and soli*ps*ist are false rhymes.

OFF-RHYME (slant rhyme) substitutes *similarity* of sound for identity of sound. Thus, bri*dge*, he*dge*, gou*ge*, enra*ge*, and even rou*ge* are slant rhymes. In effect, all vowels and vowel sounds (including diphthongs) are considered to be interchangeable, as are certain consonantal sounds that are related, such as the soft *g* in *gouge* and *enrage*, the harder *dg* in *bridge* and *hedge*, and the *zh* sound in *rouge* above.

ANALYZED RHYME is described by Edward Davison* thus: One "takes two such words as *soon* and *hide* but separates the vowel from the consonantal sounds before looking for his rhymes. The *oo* of *soon* is united with the *d* of *hide;* and the *i* of *hide* with the *h* of *soon.* This simple analysis produces the [four] rhyming sounds

oon	ine
ide	ood

as a basis for new sets of words. Thus, by means of analyzed rhyme an absolute sound relationship can be established among [four] words that have hitherto seemed alien to each other." A set of such words utilizing the sounds named above might be *croon, guide, line,* and *food.*

WRENCHED RHYME has to do with treating groups of words as though they were single words, thus: *sat on it* and *fat on it.*

A MASCULINE ENDING is a terminal measure that ends on an *accented* syllable. MASCULINE RHYME is thus the rhyming of two lines of verse with masculine endings. Also see *rising rhythms* in the section dealing with SAPPHICS.

A FEMININE ENDING is a terminal measure which ends on an *unaccented* syllable. FEMININE RHYME is thus the rhyming of two lines of verse with feminine endings. See also *falling rhythms* in the section on SAPPHICS.

LIGHT RHYME is the rhyming of one line of verse having a masculine ending with another line of verse having a feminine ending.

INTERNAL RHYME has to do with the ending of one line rhyming with a word buried in its own interior, usually the syllable before a caesura.

HEAD RHYME finds the syllables at the *beginnings* of lines rhyming.

LINKED RHYME has the *final* syllable(s) of a line rhyming with the *first* syllable(s) of the following line.

INTERLACED RHYME has a rhyme in the *middle* of the line

Some Modern Poets by Edward Lewis Davison, New York: Harper and Brothers, 1928.

which rhymes with a word also in the *middle* of a preceding or following line.

CROSS-RHYME has an end sound rhyming with a word buried in a preceding or following line.

AMPHISBAENIC RHYME is "backward" rhyme: *belated–detail; stop–pots; pets*–in*step.*

In APOCOPATED RHYME one or more syllables is dropped from the ending of *one* of a pair of rhyming words: chaingang–rain/; sing/–kingpin, etc.

In EYE RHYME words are spelled similarly but pronounced differently: *flies–homilies*, for instance.

SINGLE RHYMES are words of one syllable that rhyme; DOUBLE RHYMES are words of two syllables that rhyme; TRIPLE RHYMES have three syllables, and so forth.

ASSONANCE has to do with preserving identical accented *vowel* sounds but dispensing with identical consonant sounds. Thus, b*a*t, c*a*tch, g*a*p, m*a*d, l*a*ck, d*a*bble, and *a*nagr*a*m constitute an assonantal series. Usually assonance is used internally and in addition to rhyme when rhyme is present.

CONSONANCE is a synonym for OFF-RHYME (slant rhyme, near rhyme, etc.). The verb is CONSONATE.

ALLITERATION has to do with the repetition of initial stressed sounds, usually consonants. Thus, *t*rue, *t*utor, *t*ingle, *t*ips, *t*om-tom and *t*itillation comprise an alliterative sequence.

Euphony and *dissonance* have to do with quality of sounds, and EUPHONY means a *mingling of pleasant sounds*. Certain syllabic sounds have traditionally been adjudged to be either "pleasant" or "unpleasant." Thus, DISSONANCE means a *mingling of unpleasant sounds*, primarily hard consonants, while *euphonious* sounds would include all vowels and certain consonants, including *l*, *s*, *r*, *m*, soft *c*, and so forth. A CACOPHONY is a harsh or unpleasant mingling of sounds, both euphonious and dissonant.

Finally, REPETITION has to do with the formal re-use of words or lines of a poem. A REPETON is a whole line of verse that is formally repeated *one* other time elsewhere in the poem. A REPETEND is a line that appears more than once, but at random, unlike the REFRAIN, which is a phrase or line of verse that is formally repeated *at intervals* elsewhere in the poem. The difference between a refrain and a *burden* is that the latter is a stanza (a couplet or larger) that is repeated at intervals.

In these first chapters on metrics and sonics we have covered certain formal devices with which the poet may manipulate the *sounds* of the language in his ordering process. However, though poems may be, and have been, written utilizing only the sonic attributes of words, the poet will usually want his poem to mean something as well as be something. Therefore, in the next chapter we will talk about ways in which language may be intensified or heightened in order to achieve its fullest effects.

Chapter Three
Some Notes on Tropes

The dictionary defines *trope* as, "The use of a word or expression in a figurative sense: FIGURE OF SPEECH." Thus, a trope has to do with *figurative language*. All tropes are descriptive in nature, but not all descriptions are tropes. "One picture is worth a thousand words," the saying goes, but the poet knows that if he gets the right combination of words they may be better than a picture by a lot. Tropes are devices for intensifying descriptions. A description of a bird might be something like this: "A bird is a feathered animal having two four-clawed feet; two wings, with which most species fly; and a beak. It builds nests and hatches its young from eggs. Many birds eat insects or seeds, though some species prey on small game, carrion, or fish. . . ." A trope, however, might point out that "A bird is a live arrow."

This particular kind of trope is a METAPHOR: the *equation* of one thing with another, seemingly *unrelated* thing; yet both have at least one point in common, though that point may not be recognized easily. A SIMILE is sometimes called a "weaker metaphor"—it uses the words *like* or *as:* "A bird is *like* a live arrow."

A PUN is a play on words: two words sound alike, or nearly alike, and both meanings of the sound are used simultaneously for humorous effect, as in Hilaire Belloc's famous couplet,

> "When I am dead, I hope it may be said:
> 'His sins were scarlet, but his books were read.' "

A CONCEIT is an extended metaphor, simile, or pun, or a combination of all three; the poet extends and expands his orginal trope throughout the body of a whole poem, or a section of a poem. Poetry that does this is usually called, in the twentieth century, *metaphysical* poetry. Other elements that metaphysical poetry may utilize are irony, paradox, and wit in all its forms.

IRONY has to do with saying something, but actually meaning its opposite. For instance, in talking about a fat woman one might say, "She's a *great* girl." Here the ironical remark is also a pun.

A PARADOX is a statement that contains a contradiction that is nevertheless true, or a statement that is contrary to commonly held belief: "Freedom is the prison of rebellion," for instance, or "Winter is the Spring of contemplation."

An OXYMORON is a phrase that combines terms that are paradoxical: "sweet bitterness," "terrible beauty," etc.

All words have primary meanings, and these are called DENOTATIONS or denotative meanings. But most words also have, in certain contexts, secondary meanings, or CONNOTATIONS, and often the poet will want to "orchestrate" his poem by having both primary and secondary meanings operating simultaneously. Thus, *heart* means denotatively, "An organ of the body that pumps blood." But it can also refer to *courage*, or *love*, or to *essence*, as in the statement, "He is pure of heart." The poet, if he wishes to use the word's denotative meaning and *some* of its connotative meanings, must build a context in which those meanings can operate, but not those that he wishes to exclude. For instance, "His heart beat strongly in battle" includes the word's denotation, and its connotation *courage*, but excludes the other connotations.

There are other ways of describing, however. The most common method is, of course, by using a noun or verb plus modifiers. Some nouns are abstract. An ABSTRACTION is a nonspecificity. Such a word as *soul*, for example, may mean a number of things to various people. Other nouns are concrete; for instance, "well" may mean a hole driven into the ground for the purpose of providing water. The poet may make abstractions concrete by providing them with a context that makes them analogous to something concrete: "My soul is a dark, dry well." Such a concretion is an image.

An IMAGE, in the poetic sense, is a word picture. As you may have noted, we are now back where we started from—in a sense, all tropes are word pictures, or at least DE-

SCRIPTIONS: representations of things, feelings, actions, desires, and so forth, in language. There are a number of other ways of describing or intensifying:

A SYMBOL is some sign that represents something else. Thus, a white whale, in a specific context, might represent the enigma of existence.

An EMBLEM might be defined as a commonly held symbol —a crucifix stands for Christianity.

ALLEGORY is a method of telling a story on one level, but meaning something more general and symbolic regarding the human condition. Thus, the story of "The Ugly Duckling" is an allegory whose moral is, perhaps, that "beauty is in the eye of the beholder," or "everything turns out for the best."

PERSONIFICATION gives, on the other hand, human qualities to nonhuman things. As an example, Keats in his ode "To Autumn" addresses the season as though it were a person and says, "Who hath not seen thee oft amid thy store?/Sometimes whoever seeks abroad may find/Thee sitting careless on a granary floor,/Thy hair soft lifted by the winnowing wind; . . . "

These lines also exhibit the rhetorical technique of APOSTROPHE or direct address. The poet in his poem addresses an absent or a (usually) personified thing or abstraction.

SYNESTHESIA is talking about one of the senses in terms of another: "The morning smelled blue," "I could taste her sweet whispers," and so forth.

ONOMATOPOEIA is a method of describing something by means of sonic and rhythmical devices, making the *sound* of the language imitate the thing, i.e., "The seashore roared from the seashell's folds."

APOSIOPESIS is a way of emphasizing a word by deleting it, but making that word obvious in a context—for instance, in a couplet such as, "All men who make passes/Are nothing but . . ." the deleted word is obvious. Similarly, a word may be emphasized by changing it to another word: "All men who make passes/Are nothing but . . . donkeys."

An ALLUSION in a poem is an indirect or implied reference

to something outside the poem, or something that is not organically a part of the poem, i.e., "He came, *like Rome*, to see, and stayed to conquer."

METONYMY is description by means of a word related to that which is to be described rather than by naming the thing itself: "The *flag* will find a way to win" instead of "the *country*" or "the *government*."

SYNECHDOCHE, similar to metonymy, substitutes a part for the whole: "He was a farm *hand*" rather than "farm *worker*."

HYPERBOLE is calculated exaggeration: "Her eyes were as big as saucers."

LITOTES, the reverse of hyperbole, is studied unterstatement: "Her eyes were eyes, and they were open."

A PERIPHRASIS is a way of saying something in a more grandiose or roundabout way than is usual: "She was taken to the bosom of her fathers," for instance, instead of "she died."

An ELLIPSIS, conversely, is a way of saying something in a starker manner than is usual: "I love darkness" instead of "I am in love with darkness."

In conclusion, we ought to note the term AMBIGUITY. William Empson, in his book entitled *Seven Types of Ambiguity*,* has abstracted seven ways in which ambiguity may enhance (or, to return to an earlier suggestion, *orchestrate*) poetry. Mr. Empson describes these ambiguities thus:

1) "First type ambiguities arise when a detail is effective in several ways at once, e.g., by comparisons with several points of likeness, antitheses with several points of difference, 'comparative' adjectives, subdued metaphors, and extra meanings suggested by rhythm."

2) " . . . two or more alternative meanings are fully resolved into one."

3) " . . . two apparently unconnected meanings are given simultaneously."

*Published in the U.S. by New Directions, Inc., and by Meridian Books in 1955.

4) " . . . the alternative meanings combine to make clear a complicated state of mind in the author."

5) " . . . a fortunate confusion, as when the author is discovering his idea in the act of writing . . . or not holding it all at once."

6) " . . . what is said is contradictory or irrelevant and the reader is forced to invent interpretations."

7) " . . . full contradiction, marking a division in the author's mind."

The reader is referred to the book for more complete information and examples.

So much for the techniques of versification. It remains now for you to try your skills within some kind of construct. The remainder of *The Book of Forms* is the most complete assemblage of traditional verse forms ever collected in America, or perhaps anywhere, in one volume. Some of the forms are simple, some extremely complex. They will provide you with ample devices for testing your mastery of the language, and your growth as a *maker*.

Chapter Four
The Book of Forms

FORM-FINDER

In order to identify the form of a poem you have been reading, do the following *first;* a) determine its *meter;* b) determine its *rhyme scheme;* c) count the lines in *one stanza* (if you are looking for a stanza form) *or* the number of lines in the whole poem (if you are looking for a poem form).

When you have done these things, d) look under the appropriate heading of the Form-Finder: if the form is irregular, look under *Irregular Forms;* if the form is regular, look under *Regular Forms,* then under the appropriate sub-heading (One-Line Forms through Two-Hundred-Line Forms). If you think the form is regular, but you cannot find it listed, then check the Irregular Forms.

Under these various headings you will find lists of forms that you may look up in the body of Chapter Four, which you should compare with your poem until you find the form in which your poem is written.

REGULAR FORMS:

One-Line Forms
adonic (see *Sapphics*)
Alexandrine (see *Poulter's measure*)
Anglo-Saxon prosody
blank verse
choriambics
cyhydedd naw ban
classical hexameter (see *elegiacs*)
    classical pentameter
fourteener (see *Poulter's measure*)

free verse
  Nasher
  antithetical parallel
  climactic parallel
  synonymous parallel
  synthetic parallel
hendecasyllabics
heroic line (see *heroics*)
Hudibrastics (see *satirics*)
mote
rhupunt
Sapphic line (see *Sapphics*)
septenary (see *Poulter's measure*)
tawddgyrch cadwynog (see *rhupunt*)

Two-Line Forms
carol texte
couplet
  cyhydedd fer
  cywydd deuair fyrion
  cywydd deuair hirion
  qasida
  short couplet
  split couplet
elegiacs
heroic couplet (see *heroics*)
Hudibrastics (see *satirics*)
Poulter's measure
primer couplet (see *didactics*)
tanka couplet (see *tanka*)

Three-Line Forms
tercet
  enclosed tercet
  haiku
  Sicilian tercet
terza rima
triplet
  enclosed triplet

33

rannaigheacht ghairid (see *rannaigheachts*)
   deachnadh mór
   randaigecht chctharchubaid
   rannaigheacht bheag
   rannaigheacht mhór
rionnaird tri n-ard
rispetto stanza
rubai
Sapphics
séadna
   séadna mór
sneadhbhairdne
toddaid
wheel (see *bob and wheel*)

Five-Line Forms
ballade suprême envoy
bob and wheel
chant royal envoy
cinquain
limerick
   madsong stanza
quintet
   quintilla
   Sicilian quintet
tanka

Six-Line Forms
clogyrnach
cywydd llosgyrnog
gwawdodyn hir (see *gwawdodyn*)
hir a thoddaid
rime couée
   standard habbie
sestet
   heroic sestet
   Italian sestet
   sextilla
   Sicilian sestet

short particular measure (see *common measure*)
stave
   couplet envelope

Seven-Line Forms
rime royal
rondelet
septet
   Sicilian septet

Eight-Line Forms
ballade stanza
   ballade à double refrain stanza
   double ballade stanza
   huitain
common octave (see *common measure*)
   hymnal octave
   long hymnal octave
   long octave
   short hymnal octave
   short octave
cyhydedd hir
cyrch a chuta
lai nouveau (see *lai*)
octave
   Italian octave
   Sicilian octave
   strambotto
madrigal
ottava rima
rispetto
   heroic octave
   heroic rispetto
triolet

Nine-Line Forms
lai
   virelai
Ronsardian ode stanza
Spenserian stanza

triad (see *tercet*)

Ten-Line Forms
ballade suprême stanza
   dizain
   double ballade suprême stanza
English ode stanza (see *ode*)
glose stanza
madrigal

Eleven-Line Forms
chant royal stanza
madrigal
roundel

Twelve-Line Forms
Pearline stanza
rondeau prime (see *rondeau*)

Thirteen-Line Forms
madrigal
rondel

Fourteen-Line Forms

bref double
   quatorzain
rondel prime (see *rondel*)
sonetto rispetto (see *rispetto*)
sonnet
   English sonnet
   Italian sonnet
   Spenserian sonnet
terza rima sonnet (see *terza rima*)

Fifteen-Line Forms
rondeau

Eighteen-Line Forms
heroic sonnet (see *sonnet*)
triversen

Nineteen-Line Forms
terzanelle
villanelle

Twenty-Line Forms
caudated sonnet (see *sonnet*)

Twenty-Five-Line Forms
rondeau redoublé (see *rondeau*)

Twenty-Eight-Line Forms
ballade
    ballade à double refrain

Thirty-Line Forms
English ode (see *ode*)

Thirty-Five-Line Forms
ballade suprême (see *ballade*)

Thirty-Nine-Line Forms
sestina

Forty-Eight-Line Forms
double ballade (see *ballade*)

Sixty-Line Forms
chant royal
double ballade suprême (see *ballade*)

Ninety-Eight-Line Forms
crown of sonnets (see *sonnet*)

Two-Hundred-Line Forms
Qasida

Two-Hundred-Ten-Line Forms
sonnet redoublé (see *sonnet*)

IRREGULAR FORMS:

acrostic
    double acrostic
ballad

38

didactics
  epistle
  georgics
  riddle

dramatics
  dialogue
  eclogue
  monologue
  soliloquy
droighneach

free verse
  polyphonic prose
  prose poem

lyrics
  alba (aubade)
  anacreontics
  canso (canzo, canzone)
  canticle
  carol
  chant
  chantey
  dithyramb
  elegy (dirge, monody, threnody)
  epithalamion
  lay
  madrigal
  madsong
  nursery rhyme
  pastoral (idyl)
  pastoral elegy
  prothalamion
  riddle
  romance
  roundelay
  rune
  serenade
  sirvente

ode
    homostrophic ode
    irregular (Cowleyan) ode
    Pindaric ode
palinode
satirics
    epigram
    epitaph
    Skeltonics
spatials (calligramme, hieroglyphic verse, shaped stanza)
    concrete verse

ACROSTIC

May be in any of the meters or in any form. What is of primary importance is that the first letters of all lines, when read downward, spell out a word or a phrase, usually a name. The DOUBLE ACROSTIC repeats this feat with the last letters of the lines as well.

A typical scheme:

lines:	first letter of first word:
1.	J-
2.	O-
3.	H-
4.	N-
5.	D-
6.	O-
7.	E-

Note that separate words usually form separate stanzas.

A scheme for a double acrostic:

lines:	first and last letters:	
1.	E-	-e
2.	V-	-v
3.	E-	-e
4.	R-	-r
5.	Y-	-y
6.	M-	-m
7.	A-	-a
8.	N-	-n
9.	I-	-i
10.	N-	-n
11.	L-	-l
12.	O-	-o
13.	V-	-v
14.	E-	-e

See also the RUNE in the LYRICS section.

41

AE FREISLIGHE

Irish. Syllabic.

Since this is the first of the Celtic forms to be encountered in *The Book of Forms*, perhaps a note is in order. Almost all of the Irish and Welsh forms are very complex systems of rhyme, alliteration, and consonance (called, collectively, *cynghanedd*). For the practical purpose of versification in English it should be understood that the systems are almost impossible to reproduce accurately in our language. Therefore, perhaps it would be as well for the poet attempting these forms to pay most attention only to the rhyme scheme and syllabification. Thus, ae freislighe simplified would be a QUATRAIN stanza of seven-syllable lines. Lines *one* and *three* rhyme in triple rhymes; lines *two* and *four* rhyme in double rhymes.

The *poem* (not the stanza) should end with the same first syllable, word, or line with which it begins. The technical term for this ending is *dúnadh*, and it occurs in all the Gaelic forms.

The diagram:

lines:	syllables and rhymes:
1.	x x x x x̲ x̲ a
2.	x x x x x x̲ b̲
3.	x x x x x̲ x̲ a
4.	x x x x x x̲ b̲

This form should not be confused with the SICILIAN QUATRAIN, which has a similar rhyme scheme.

ALCAICS

Greek. Accentual-syllabic. Unrhymed. A QUATRAIN stanza. The first two lines consist of an acephalous iamb, two trochees, and two dactyls, in that order; the third line consists of an acephalous iamb and four trochees, in that order; the fourth line is made of two dactyls followed by two trochees.

The pattern:

lines:	meters:				
1.	x́	x́x	x́x	x́xx	x́xx
2.	x́	x́x	x́x	x́xx	x́xx
3.	x́	x́x	x́x	x́x	x́x
4.	x́xx	x́xx	x́x	x́x	

Accentual. A LINE utilizing alliteration and stress. It is composed of two half-lines separated by a *caesura* or rhythmic pause. Each half-line is called a *hemistich* and owns two accented syllables. Thus, there are *four accents to the full line*. There may be *any number of unaccented syllables* in a line.

The *initial sounds* of the first three *accented syllables* are alliterated. Though exactly the same *consonant* sounds must be alliterated, any *vowel* may "alliterate" with any other vowel: actually, what is being alliterated in the latter case is the *absence* of consonants.

Although it is *not a requirement* of the form, the alliteration *may* at times be continued into the fourth accented syllable. Also, sometimes the *fourth* accented syllable of a line becomes the alliteration in the following line.

Here is a diagram of some possible lines of Anglo-Saxon prosody:

lines:	words, syllables, alliterations, accents, caesuras:
1.	xx áxx x áx • á xxxx b́x x
2.	ćxxx xxx ć • ćx x d́xx
3.	d́x d́xx • d́ xxx d́
4.	xx xxx é x éx • x éxx fx
5.	etcetera.

See also the PEARLINE STANZA and *sprung rhythm*. For a form sometimes associated with Anglo-Saxon prosody, see the BOB AND WHEEL.

AWDL GYWYDD

Welsh. Syllabic. A QUATRAIN stanza of seven-syllable lines. Lines *two* and *four* rhyme; lines one and three *cross-rhyme into* the third, fourth, *or* fifth *syllable* of lines two and four.

Here is a possible scheme for three stanzas of awdl gywydd:

lines:	syllables and rhymes:
1.	x x x x x x a
2.	x x *a* *x* *x* x b
3.	x x x x x x c
4.	x x *x* *x* *c* x b
5.	x x x x x x d
6.	x x *x* *d* *x* x e
7.	x x x x x x f
8.	x x *x* *f* *x* x e
9.	x x x x x x g
10.	x x *x* *x* *g* x h
11.	x x x x x x i
12.	x x *x* *i* *x* x h
13.	etcetera.

BALLAD

Universal in the western world. Usually accentual-syllabic. The BALLAD STANZA is often $a^4b^3c^4b^3$: here the letters stand for rhymes, the numbers stand for the number of metrical feet to a line. The ballad is not, however, a fixed form. It may be written in any meter. Often it is rhymed, and *internal rhyme* is sometimes used. There is no fixed stanza or line length, and it often has a *refrain* or *burden*. Meant to be sung, the ballad may be defined as a *lyrical* verse *narrative*, for ballads tell stories.

Here is a possible pattern for one loose anapestic ballad stanza with internal rhymes and refrain:

lines:	*meters, rhymes, refrain:*
1.	xxx́ xá xxx́ xxá
2.	xx́ xxx́ xb́
3.	xxx́ xxć xxx́ xxć
4.	xxx́ xxx́ xB́—*refrain*

For related forms see COMMON MEASURE. For other narrative forms see the LAY and ROMANCE in the section on LYRICS, the EPIC in the section on HEROICS, and the FABLIAU in the section titled VERSE NARRATIVES.

A distinction is often made between the FOLK BALLAD, which is traditional and anonymous, and the LITERARY BALLAD, which is a composition by a known author. The former often manifests a phenomenon called "leaping and lingering," which means that the folk ballad skips from high point to high point, ignoring details of the narrative, whereas the literary ballad develops the whole narrative, including details and climaxes. For more information concerning the metric of the ballad, see *dipodics*.

BALLADE

A French form. Syllabic. Lines may be of any length, but are usually of eight or ten syllables. Twenty-eight lines divided in three OCTAVE stanzas and one QUATRAIN half-stanza, which is called the *envoi* or *envoy*. The ballade turns on three rhymes and is built on a *refrain*, which appears as the last line of each stanza and of the envoy.

Here is the scheme for the first stanza:

lines:	rhymes:
1.	a
2.	b
3.	a
4.	b
5.	b
6.	c
7.	b
8.	C—*refrain*

The second stanza (lines nine through sixteen) and the third stanza (lines seventeen through twenty-four) are exactly the same. Here is the scheme for the envoy:

25.	b
26.	c
27.	b
28.	C—*refrain*

Note well: there are only *three rhymes in the whole poem*, and no rhyme or rhyme word should be repeated.

The BALLADE SUPRÈME has thirty-five lines: three ten-line stanzas rhyming ababbccdcD with an envoy of five lines rhyming ccdcD. The refrain appears as the last line of each stanza and of the envoy. Note that this form has four rhymes.

The DOUBLE BALLADE and the DOUBLE BALLADE SUPRÊME have six stanzas of either eight or ten lines respectively and follow the rhyme schemes of the ballade and the ballade suprême. An envoy is *optional;* if one is used, it is the same as in the ballade and ballade suprême. The refrain appears as the last line of each stanza and of the envoy.

The BALLADE À DOUBLE REFRAIN has three eight-line stanzas rhyming abaBbcbC with an envoy of four lines rhyming bBcC. It has two refrains. The first refrain appears as lines four, twelve, twenty, and twenty-six; the second refrain appears as lines eight, sixteen, twenty-four, and twenty-eight.

The CHANT ROYAL, a member of the ballade family, is listed separately.

The HUITAIN is a complete poem composed of one ballade stanza (*ababbcbc*); Huitains used as stanzas are called MONK'S TALE STANZA. The DIZAIN is a complete poem composed of one ballade suprême stanza (*ababbccdcd*). The lines are either eight or ten syllables in length for both forms (in English metrics, iambic tetrameter or pentameter).

Note that the addition of an *Alexandrine* line to the iambic pentameter huitain, to form a final couplet, will result in one SPENSERIAN STANZA: *ababbcbcc*[6].

BLANK VERSE

Accentual-syllabic. Strictly speaking, blank verse is a LINE of any unrhymed, *metered* verse. However, it is more commonly understood to mean *unrhymed iambic pentameter verse*. Note that *free verse is not blank verse;* blank verse is *metered*, free verse is not.

line: *meters:*
1.   xx́ xx́ xx́ xx́ xx́

See also HEROICS.

BOB AND WHEEL

The "bob and wheel" is an English *accentual-syllabic* QUINTET *stanza* that is sometimes found in association with *accentual* poems. Specifically, it is a *metrical tail* on a stanza of Anglo-Saxon prosody.

The final line of the *accentual stanza* proper is usually a run-on line that is continued by the BOB: a line of verse composed of one *or* two verse feet—sometimes of only one accented syllable. The bob itself may be a run-on line that is continued and completed by the WHEEL: four lines, each of which consists of *three* verse feet.

The *bob* rhymes with lines *two* and *four* of the wheel; lines *one* and *three* of the wheel rhyme with each other.

This is the structure of the entire bob and wheel:

lines:	meters and rhymes:		
1.	... xx	xá	
2.	xx́	xx́	xb́
3.	xx́	xx́	xá
4.	xx́	xx́	xb́
5.	xx́	xx́	xá

For the form with which it is most commonly associated, see ANGLO-SAXON PROSODY.

BREF DOUBLE

French. Syllabic. Lines may be of any length. Fourteen lines arranged in three QUATRAIN stanzas and a concluding COUPLET. There are only three rhymes in the poem, but not every line is rhymed. The *a* rhyme appears twice somewhere within the three quatrains and once in the couplet. The *b* rhyme does likewise. The *c* rhyme ends each quatrain. A possible scheme:

lines:	*rhymes:*
1.	a
2.	x—*no rhyme*
3.	b
4.	c
5.	x—*no rhyme*
6.	b
7.	x—*no rhyme*
8.	c
9.	x—*no rhyme*
10.	a
11.	x—*no rhyme*
12.	c
13.	a
14.	b

This form is thought to be an ancestor of the SONNET. Actually, the bref double is a QUATORZAIN: any stanza or poem of fourteen lines *other than* a sonnet. Other quatorzains with set forms are the SONETTO RISPETTO and the TERZA RIMA sonnet.

BYR A THODDAID

Welsh. Syllabic. This QUATRAIN *stanza* combines a COUPLET consisting of eight syllables per line with another COUPLET consisting of ten syllables in the *first* line and six syllables in the *second* line. In the *ten-syllable line* the *main rhyme* is found *before* the end of the line, and the syllables that *follow* the main rhyme in the ten-syllable line must be *linked* by means of alliteration, assonance, or *secondary rhyme* with the *early syllables* of the first part of the *six-syllable* line. In the quatrain either couplet may follow the other.

Note that in this scheme primary or *main rhymes are in capital letters;* alliteration, assonances, or *secondary rhymes are indicated by means of small letters:*

lines:	syllables and rhymes:
1.	x x x x x x x A
2.	x x x x x x x A
3.	x x x x x x x B x c
4.	x c x x x B
5.	x x x x x x D x x e
6.	e x x x x D
7.	x x x x x x x F
8.	x x x x x x x F
9.	etcetera.

CAROL

French and English. Generally speaking, a carol is simply a "joyous hymn" (see p. 80). However, it originally had a more-or-less set form that consisted of a two-line *burden* or *texte* COUPLET rhyming A^1A^2, and any number of QUATRAIN stanzas rhyming *bbba*. The last lines of these stanzas rhymed with the burden, or they echoed or repeated one or the other of the burden lines. Usually the meter was short, trimeter or tetrameter; no set verse foot. The whole burden might be repeated at intervals.

A possible scheme:

lines:	meters, rhymes, refrains:
1.	xx́ xx́ xx́ xÁ¹ ⎞
2.	xx́ xx́ xx́ xÁ² ⎠ TEXTE (burden)
3.	xx́ xx́ xx́ xb́
4.	xx́ xx́ xx́ xb́
5.	xx́ xx́ xx́ xb́
6.	xx́ xx́ xx́ xá or A¹ or A²
7.	xx́ xx́ xx́ xć
8.	xx́ xx́ xx́ xć
9.	xx́ xx́ xx́ xć
10.	xx́ xx́ xx́ xá or A¹ or A²
11.	xx́ xx́ xx́ xÁ¹
12.	xx́ xx́ xx́ xÁ²
13.	etcetera.

For other forms that use a *texte*, see the GLOSE, the RONDEAU REDOUBLÉ, and the SONNET REDOUBLÉ.

CASBAIRDNE

Irish. Syllabic. A QUATRAIN *stanza* of heptasyllabic lines
with trisyllabic endings. Lines *two* and *four* rhyme, and lines
one and *three* consonate (not rhyme) with them. There are
at least two *cross-rhymes* in each couplet; in the first couplet
these need *not* be exact. There is alliteration as in RAN-
NAIGHEACHT MHÓR, the final syllable of line *four* alliterating
with the *preceding stressed word*.

The *poem* (not the stanza) ends with the same first syllable,
word, or line with which it begins.

A simplified version:

lines:	syllables and rhymes:						
1.	x	*x*	b	*x*	x	x	a
2.	x	*a*	*x*	*x*	x	x	b
3.	x	*x*	*x*	b	x	x	c
4.	x	*x*	c	*x*	x	x	d

—*consonate* (lines 1–2)

—*consonate* (lines 3–4)

54

CHANT ROYAL

A French form. Syllabic. Lines may be of any length. Sixty lines divided into five eleven-line stanzas and one five-line *envoy*. The chant royal turns on five rhymes and is built on a *refrain*. Strictly speaking, it is a form of the BALLADE.

This is the scheme of *all* stanzas:

lines:	rhymes:
1.	a
2.	b
3.	a
4.	b
5.	c
6.	c
7.	d
8.	d
9.	e
10.	d
11.	E—*refrain*

and this is the scheme of the *envoy:*

56.	d
57.	d
58.	e
59.	d
60.	E—*refrain*

CHORIAMBICS

Greek. Accentual-syllabic. A LINE consisting, in this order, of two trochees, an iamb, a trochee, an iamb, a trochee, and two iambs. Unrhymed. Poems may consist of any number of lines.

Scheme for one line:

line: *meters:*
  1. x́x x́x xx́ x́x xx́ x́x xx́ xx́

CINQUAIN

An American form. Syllabic or accentual-syllabic. Five lines long, the lines consist of two, four, six, eight, and two syllables respectively. It is unrhymed, a set form of the QUINTET.

Originally the poem was written in iambs: one iambic foot in the first line, two in the second, three in the third, four in the fourth, and one in the fifth line.

Here is the scheme in syllabics:

lines: *syllables:*
  1. x x
  2. x x x x
  3. x x x x x x
  4. x x x x x x x x
  5. x x

For similar forms see the HAIKU in the section dealing with the TERCET, and the TANKA.

CLOGYRNACH

A Welsh form. Syllabic. A SESTET *stanza* having lines with counts of eight, eight, five, five, three, and three syllables respectively. The two three-syllable lines may, if desired, be written as one six-syllable line. The rhyme scheme is *aabbba*.

A diagram of one stanza of clogyrnach is as follows:

lines:	*syllables and rhymes:*
1.	x x x x x x x a
2.	x x x x x x x a
3.	x x x x b
4.	x x x x b
5.	x x b
6.	x x a
7.	etcetera.

COMMON MEASURE

Accentual-syllabic. Rhymed. A QUATRAIN *stanza* written in strict iambics, unlike the BALLAD *stanza*, which is otherwise similar. The rhyme scheme is *abcb*. The *first* and *third* lines consist of four iambic feet; the *second* and *fourth* lines of three iambic feet. Thus, a simple scheme of the stanza might be written $a^4b^3c^4b^3$.

A complete scheme:

lines:	*meters and rhymes:*		
1.	xx́	xx́	xx́	xá
2.	xx́	xx́	xb́
3.	xx́	xx́	xx́	xć
4.	xx́	xx́	xb́

HYMNAL STANZA is the same except that it rhymes *abab*.

SHORT MEASURE, a form of common measure, appears thus: $a^3b^3c^4b^3$; SHORT HYMNAL STANZA is similar: $a^3b^3a^4b^3$. LONG MEASURE rhymes *abcb*, but all lines are iambic tetrameter, as are the lines in LONG HYMNAL STANZA, which rhymes *abab*.

All forms of common measure and hymnal stanza may be doubled to make OCTAVE stanzas. These are called COMMON OCTAVE, HYMNAL OCTAVE, SHORT OCTAVE, SHORT HYMNAL OCTAVE, LONG OCTAVE, and LONG HYMNAL OCTAVE.

SHORT PARTICULAR MEASURE is a SESTET *stanza* that has three iambic feet in lines *one, two, four,* and *five;* and four feet in lines *three* and *six.* It usually rhymes $a^3a^3b^4a^3a^3b^4$. For a reversal of this pattern see RIME COUÉE.

COUPLET

Any two lines, written as a unit. May be in any length and in any meter. Most couplets rhyme *aa*. There are several set forms.

The SHORT COUPLET is written in either *iambic* or *trochaic tetrameter*. The pattern in iambics:

lines:	meters and rhymes:
1.	xx́ xx́ xx́ xá
2.	xx́ xx́ xx́ xá

The SPLIT COUPLET is also accentual-syllabic. It consists of two lines, the *first* of which is written in *iambic pentameter* measures, the *second* in iambic dimeter:

| 1. | xx́ xx́ xx́ xx́ xá |
| 2. | xx́ xá |

There are three Welsh couplets, all of them syllabic.

CYHYDEDD FER is a rhymed couplet, of which each line contains eight syllables.

CYWYDD DEUAIR FYRION has each line containing four syllables, and it is rhymed.

CYWYDD DEUAIR HIRION is a light-rhyming couplet—that is, the first line is masculine, ending on a stressed or *accented syllable*, and the second line is feminine, ending on an un-stressed or *unaccented syllable*, and the lines rhyme *aa*. A schematic for two couplets:

lines:	syllables, rhymes, accents:
1.	x́ x x́ x x́ x á
2.	x́ x x́ x x x́ a
3.	x́ x x́ x́ x x b́
4.	x x́ x x́ x x́ b

Note that each line of cywydd deuair hirion contains seven syllables, and that the accents need not be regular (metrical).

The QASĪDA, an Arabic form, consists of any number of couplets, up to one hundred, all turning on the same rhyme.

For other set forms of the couplet see the sections on DIDACTICS, FREE VERSE, HEROICS, and POULTER'S MEASURE.

CYHYDEDD HIR

Welsh. Syllabic. OCTAVE *stanzas* composed of two QUA-TRAINS each of whose four lines consist of five, five, five, and four, syllables respectively. Each quatrain may, if desired, be arranged as a single nineteen-syllable line. The five-syllable lines in each quatrain rhyme with one another; the four-syllable lines carry the *main rhyme*.

Strictly speaking, the stanzas need *not* be octave stanzas. Any number of quatrains may be used in a stanza and technically the meter will remain cyhydedd hir. However, within any stanza the short lines must carry the same rhyme.

Scheme of two octave stanzas:

lines:	syllables and rhymes:
1.	x x x x a
2.	x x x x a
3.	x x x x a
4.	x x x B
5.	x x x x c
6.	x x x x c
7.	x x x x c
8.	x x x B
9.	x x x x d
10.	x x x x d
11.	x x x x d
12.	x x x E
13.	x x x x f
14.	x x x x f
15.	x x x x f
16.	x x x E
17.	etcetera.

CYHYDEDD NAW BAN

Welsh. Syllabic. A LINE of nine syllables. It *must* rhyme with at least one other line of equal length to form a couplet. However, it may continue the rhyme throughout the stanza, which may be of any length, provided that all lines are equal in length.

The scheme for three lines:

lines:	syllables and rhymes:
1.	x x x x x x x x a
2.	x x x x x x x x a
3.	x x x x x x x x a
4.	etcetera.

This form should not be confused with the QASIDA.

CYRCH A CHUTA

Welsh. Syllabic. An OCTAVE *stanza* of six rhyming or slant-rhyming seven-syllable lines plus a couplet, the *second* line of which rhymes with the first six lines. The first line of the couplet (line seven) *cross-rhymes into* the third, fourth, or fifth syllable of line eight.

The scheme for one stanza:

lines:	syllables and rhymes:
1.	x x x x x x a
2.	x x x x x x a
3.	x x x x x x a
4.	x x x x x x a
5.	x x x x x x a
6.	x x x x x x a
7.	x x x x x x b
8.	x x *x b x* x a
9.	etcetera.

CYWYDD LLOSGYRNOG

A Welsh form. Syllabic. A SESTET *stanza*, the lines having respective syllable counts of eight, eight, seven, eight, eight, and seven syllables. Lines *one* and *two* rhyme, and cross-rhyme with the *middle* syllable of line *three*; lines *four* and *five* rhyme, and cross-rhyme with the *middle* syllable of line *six*; lines *three* and *six* rhyme with each other.

Here is the schematic for a stanza:

lines:	syllables and rhymes:
1.	x x x x x x x a
2.	x x x x x x x a
3.	x x x *a* x x b
4.	x x x x x x x c
5.	x x x x x x x c
6.	x x x *c* x x b
7.	etcetera.

This form should not be confused with RIME COUÉE, which has a similar rhyme scheme.

DEIBHIDHE

Irish. Syllabic. A QUATRAIN *stanza* light-rhyming in couplets. There is alliteration between two words in each line, the final word of line *four* alliterating with the preceding stressed word. There are at least two cross-rhymes between lines *three* and *four*. Each line has seven syllables.

The *poem* (not the stanza) ends with the same first syllable, word, or line with which it begins.

The diagram for one stanza:

lines:	syllables, rhymes; accented endings:
1.	x x x x x x á
2.	x x x x x x́ a
3.	x b x x x x b́
4.	x x x b x x́ b

DIDACTICS

There are four didactic forms in English prosody.

The EPISTLE is a loose form. It is a letter to someone or to mankind in general, and it serves as a medium for hortatory instruction.

The PRIMER COUPLET, a set form, is a dipodic (two-verse-foot) couplet rhyming *aa*. Essentially, primer couplets are rhymed aphorisms.

A scheme for a primer couplet in iambs:

lines:	*meters and rhymes:*	
1.	xx́	xá
2.	xx́	xá

The RIDDLE is a short lyric that poses a question, the answer to which lies hidden in hints.

GEORGICS are rhymed instructions or directions in the arts, sciences, or trades; versified handbooks.

DRAMATICS

There are three loose verse forms which can exist outside the drama proper.

A DIALOGUE is a conversation in verse among two or more characters.

The MONOLOGUE (or *dramatic monologue*, as it is sometimes called) is a verse speech by a single character. However, a listening audience is assumed, and the speaker addresses himself to his listeners (the reader or a silent character).

The SOLILOQUY is similar, but the speaker is assumed to be alone, and his speech consists of his private thoughts verbalized.

A fourth form is not, specifically speaking, a dramatic form. The ECLOGUE (or *bucolic*) is really a PASTORAL (see the section on LYRICS). However, it is cast in the form of a dialogue between two herdsmen or shepherds.

DROIGHNEACH

Irish. Syllabic. A loose *stanza* form. The single line may consist of from nine to thirteen syllables, and it *always* ends in a trisyllabic word. There is rhyme between lines *one* and *three*, *two* and *four*, etc. There are at least two cross-rhymes in each couplet. There is alliteration in each line—usually the final word of the line alliterates with the preceding stressed word, and it *always* does so in the *last* line of each stanza. Stanzas may consist of any number of quatrains.

The *poem* (not the stanza) ends with the same first syllable, word, or line with which it begins.

A possible scheme:

lines:	syllables and rhymes:
1.	x x b x x x x x <u>x x a</u>
2.	x x x x a x x x x <u>x x b</u>
3.	x x x x x b x x <u>a</u>
4.	x x x x a x x <u>x x b</u>
5.	x x x x x d x x <u>x x c</u>
6.	x x x c x x x x x x <u>x x d</u>
7.	x x d x x x x x x <u>x x c</u>
8.	x x x x c x <u>x x d</u>
9.	etcetera.

ELEGIACS

Greek. Accentual-syllabic. A COUPLET measure. The *first line* is a CLASSICAL HEXAMETER: the *first four* feet are either spondees or dactyls, the *fifth* foot is a dactyl, the *sixth* is a spondee.

The *second line* of the couplet is a CLASSICAL PENTAMETER, which consists, in this order, of *two* dactyls, a spondee, and *two* anapests. It may be rhymed or unrhymed.

A possible scheme:

lines:	*meters:*					
1.	x́xx	x́xx	x́xx	x́xx	x́xx	x́x́
2.	x́xx	x́xx	x́x́	xxx́	xxx́	

See also the ELEGY and PASTORAL ELEGY in the section on LYRICS.

Welsh. Syllabic. There are eight englyns. Six of them, those treated in this section, are QUATRAIN *stanzas*.

ENGLYN CYRCH has seven syllables in each line. Lines *one* and *two* and *four* turn on a single rhyme. Line *three* cross-rhymes *into* one of the three central syllables of line *four:*

lines:	syllables and rhymes:
1.	x x x x x x a
2.	x x x x x x a
3.	x x x x x x b
4.	x x *x x b* x a
5.	etcetera.

Each line of ENGLYN LLEDDFBROEST *diphthong-rhymes* with the others and has a count of seven syllables. In Welsh, the rhymes used were the four diphthongs *ae, oe, wy,* and *ei.* Since this is impossible to reproduce in English, any *similar diphthongs* may be substituted and may be considered to rhyme with one another. A one stanza schematic:

lines:	syllables and diphthong-rhymes:
1.	x x x x x x oe
2.	x x x x x x wy
3.	x x x x x x ei
4.	x x x x x x ae
5.	etcetera.

ENGLYN PROEST DALGRON has in each line a count of seven syllables. The lines *off-rhyme* on vowels or similar diphthongs. A possible scheme:

lines:	syllables and off-rhymes:
1.	x x x x x x oi
2.	x x x x x x ay
3.	x x x x x x ou
4.	x x x x x x uy
5.	etcetera.

In ENGLYN PROEST GADWYNOG each line has seven syllables. Lines *one* and *three* rhyme; lines *two* and *four* off-rhyme with lines *one* and *three* and with each other:

lines:	syllables, off-rhymes, and rimes:
1.	x x x x x x r
2.	x x x x x x or
3.	x x x x x x r
4.	x x x x x x or
5.	etcetera.

ENGLYN UNODL CRWCA has lines that have syllable counts of seven, seven, ten, and six respectively. Lines *one*, *two*, and *four end* with the *main* rhyme. In line *three* the main rhyme is followed by one, two, or three *syllables* that are *echoed* by assonance, alliteration, *or* secondary rhyme in the first part of the *fourth* line:

lines:	syllables and rhymes:
1.	x x x x x x A
2.	x x x x x x A
3.	x x x x x x A *x* *x* *b*
4.	*x* *b* *x* x x A
5.	etcetera.

ENGLYN UNODL UNION merely shifts the positions of the two couplets that make up englyn unodl crwca: lines *three* and *four* of the latter become lines *one* and *two*, and lines *one* and *two* become lines *three* and *four* of the englyn unodl union.

Two other englyns will be found in the section on TRIPLETS.

FREE VERSE

The term "free verse" is derived from the French *vers libre*, which Ezra Pound, Amy Lowell, and others began to popularize during the 'teens and 'twenties of this century, in the pages of Harriet Monroe's *Poetry* magazine and elsewhere. But as it is applied to English prosodies, the term is misleading, if not actually inapplicable.

As one may easily see, in looking through the forms of this book, the French prosodic system is syllabic, not accentual. The reason for this is that the French consider their language to be *without* stresses; thus, they are precluded from using any accentual or metrical (accentual-syllabic) system. It should be clear, then, that if the French refrain from writing lines that contain specific numbers of syllables, their verse is "free." However, this is *not* the case with verse written in English.

The English language is emphatically a stressed language —we can hear the cadences of our words. It has been said, in fact, that English is basically an iambic language. And we say, further, that any English-language poet, whether he be a "free verse" poet or otherwise, must have an "ear" . . . that is, an ear for cadences.

Therefore, it should be obvious that English poetry can never be "free" in the sense that French poetry may be *libre*. No matter what the English-speaking poet may do, his verse will be basically accentual (though he may use other systems *besides* accentuals). In fact, one might go so far as to point out that *most free verse poems in English are basically iambic, or mixtures of iambic and anapestic meters.*

Finally, it comes down to this: the term "free verse," as it is applied to poetry in English, is a misnomer that has clouded the issue for years. A term such as "random metrics," denoting a certain variation in lengths of lines and liberty of substitution, is much more appropriate. Any so-called "free verse poem" in English can be scanned, and it will be evident that, more often than not, it will be an iambic, or iambic-anapestic, poem. In those cases where it is not, the poem will be seen to fit into some other system of accentual verse, such as the *variable foot*, or *dipodics*, *Skeltonics*, or perhaps *sprung rhythm* or *Anglo-Saxon prosody*.

Many poets have said that there is no such thing as "free verse." That is true, especially in English, but we have the term, and for the time being, at least, we must use it.

Free verse, then, is a LINE of verse that does not fit into one of the three *metrical* prosodic systems, yet is distinguished from prose by its more emphatic rhythms. Free verse may also utilize alliteration, consonance, various kinds of rhymes, and other devices of versification. Note that free verse is *not* blank verse: the latter is measured, the former is not measured. Lines may be of any length, and they usually vary within a poem. The line length is often determined by the *breath pause:* logical and/or vocal phraseology.

The PROSE POEM is a poem written in prose rhythms, but whose language and imagery are heightened or intensified. POLYPHONIC PROSE may utilize other devices as well, such as assonance, internal rhyme, alliteration, etcetera, but its rhythms remain those of prose, and the poem is written in paragraphs, not lines.

The VERSE PARAGRAPH is to be distinguished from the paragraphs of a prose poem. It is a unit of lines in a metrical poem that is analogous to a paragraph of prose in that it deals with matters that have logical relationships with one another and a common focus.

NASHERS are *lines* or *couplets*, usually long, of flat free verse or prose with humorous, often multisyllabic endings utilizing wrenched rhymes. Nashers are often used satirically. For another satiric form built on an opposite metric, see SKEL-TONICS in the section concerned with SATIRICS.

The systems of Hebrew prosody have been part of our tradition at least since the King James version of the Bible was introduced. A good portion of the Bible is written in verse that, since its structure does not depend upon any kind of metric, would therefore be considered *free verse* in our system, but might better be called *grammatics*.

Hebrew prosody is structured on *parallelism*. Briefly, there are four major parallelisms:

I. SYNONYMOUS PARALLELISM—Each *verse* is broken into two halves. The first half is a complete thought; the second half *repeats* the first thought using *different words*.

II. SYNTHETIC PARALLELISM—Each *verse* is broken into two halves. The first half is a complete thought; the second half gives a *consequence* of the first thought.

III. ANTITHETICAL PARALLELISM—Each *verse* is broken into two halves. The first half is a complete thought; the second half *rebuts* the first thought.

IV. CLIMACTIC PARALLELISM—Each *verse* builds upon the preceding verse until a *climax* is attained in the last verse.

Although all poetic devices may appear in parallel construction, they are not an integral part of the system, and rhyme especially will be random, if not simply accidental.

WORD-COUNT PROSODY is a free-verse system in which each line of the first stanza is assigned a certain number of words. Succeeding stanzas retain the same word-counts as the first stanza, line for line. The system is capable of great flexibility, for syllabic lengths and number of stresses in each line may vary greatly, even in lines containing the same number of words.

GLOSE

Spanish and Portuguese. Accentual-syllabic. May be written in any meter and in any line-length. The glose *begins* with a QUATRAIN called the *texte*. There are four ensuing stanzas of ten lines each: the poem is thus forty-four lines long. Each line of the texte becomes a *refrain:* in order, line one finishes stanza one; line two finishes stanza two; line three finishes stanza three, and line four finishes stanza four, completing the poem.

The only rhyme requirement is that the *sixth* and *ninth* lines of each stanza rhyme with the refrains for that stanza; the rest of the rhyme pattern is set by the poet.

The diagram for a poem with a texte rhyming *ABAB*:

lines:	rhymes and refrains:
1.	A^1 ⎫
2.	B^1 ⎪
3.	A^2 ⎬ —*texte*
4.	B^2 ⎭
5.	
6.	
7.	
8.	
9.	
10.	a
11.	
12.	
13.	a
14.	A^1—*refrain*
15.	
16.	
17.	
18.	
19.	
20.	b

21.
22.
23.   b
24.   B¹—*refrain*

25.
26.
27.
28.
29.
30.   a
31.
32.
33.   a
34.   A²—*refrain*

35.
36.
37.
38.
39.
40.   b
41.
42.
43.   b
44.   B²—*refrain*

For similar forms see the RONDEAU REDOUBLÉ, the SONNET REDOUBLÉ, and the CAROL.

GWAWDODYNS

GWAWDODYN, a syllabic Welsh form, is a QUATRAIN *stanza* that has lines of nine, nine, ten, and nine syllables respectively. The *first*, *second*, and *fourth* lines end-rhyme with one another. The *third* line may rhyme internally with itself *or* there may be a syllable *before the end of the line* that rhymes *into* line *four*.

Here are two possible stanza schemes. The first method would be diagrammed thus:

lines: *syllables and rhymes:*
1.   x x x x x x x x a
2.   x x x x x x x x a
3.   x x x x *b* x x x x b
4.   x x x x x x x x a

5.   etcetera.

The second method, which is looser, might be plotted this way:

1.   x x x x x x x x a
2.   x x x x x x x x a
3.   x x x x x x *b* *x* *x* x
4.   *x* *x* *x* *b* x x x x a

GWAWDODYN HIR is similar except that a rhyming quatrain, each line of which contains nine syllables, is substituted for the opening couplet. Thus, instead of two lines rhyming *aa*, there would be four lines rhyming *aaaa* beginning the stanza, which would then be a SESTET.

HENDECASYLLABICS

Greek. Accentual-syllabic. A pentameter LINE of eleven syllables. Strictly, it is made up, in this order, of a trochee *or* spondee, a dactyl, and three trochees *or* two trochees and a spondee:

line: *meters:*
1.   x́x x́xx x́x x́x x́x

or:

2.   x́x́ x́xx x́x x́x x́x́

HEROICS

English or Greek. Accentual-syllabic. The ENGLISH HEROIC LINE is iambic pentameter (see BLANK VERSE). A COUPLET *stanza* in this meter rhymed *aa* is called a HEROIC COUPLET. If the stanza is a QUATRAIN in this meter, it is called the HEROIC STANZA, set forms of which are the ITALIAN and the SICILIAN QUATRAIN.

The CLASSICAL HEROIC LINE is the hexameter (see ELEGIACS).

Verses composed in either of these meters are called HEROIC VERSE.

The pattern for the heroic couplet:

lines: *meters and rhymes:*
1.   xx́ xx́ xx́ xx́ xá
2.   xx́ xx́ xx́ xx́ xá

Traditionally, the greatest heroic form is the EPIC, which is a narrative poem of great length dealing with matters of large import and grand proportion.

For other heroic forms see HEROIC OCTAVE and HEROIC RISPETTO in the section dealing with the RISPETTO, the heroic SESTET and SONNET, and CHANSON DE GESTE.

HIR A THODDAID

Welsh. Syllabic. A SESTET *stanza*. Line five has a count of ten syllables. The other five lines each contain nine syllables. Lines one, two, three, four, and six rhyme. A syllable toward the end of line five cross-rhymes *into* the middle of line six.
Scheme:

lines:	*syllables and rhymes:*
1.	x x x x x x x x a
2.	x x x x x x x x a
3.	x x x x x x x x a
4.	x x x x x x x x a
5.	x x x x x x *x b x x*
6.	x x x *b x x* x x a
7.	etcetera.

KYRIELLE

French. Syllabic. A poem written in QUATRAIN *stanzas*. Each line has a count of eight syllables. The last line of the first quatrain is the *refrain*, and it reappears as the last line of each quatrain. Usually it is rhymed. The poem may have any number of stanzas.

A possible plot:

lines:	*syllables and rhymes:*
1.	x x x x x x x a
2.	x x x x x x x b
3.	x x x x x x x a
4.	x x x x x x x B—*refrain*
5.	x x x x x x x c
6.	x x x x x x x b
7.	x x x x x x x c
8.	x x x x x x x B—*refrain*
9.	etcetera.

A French form or stanza pattern. Syllabic. A poem *or* stanza of nine lines turning on two rhymes: *aabaabaab*. The *a* lines are five syllables long; the *b* lines are two syllables long.

In a poem consisting of more than one stanza, following stanzas have their own rhymes.

A diagram for one stanza:

lines:	syllables and rhymes:
1.	x x x x a
2.	x x x x a
3.	x b
4.	x x x x a
5.	x x x x a
6.	x b
7.	x x x x a
8.	x x x x a
9.	x b

The LAI NOUVEAU, also French and syllabic, is a development of the *lai*. More complicated than the *lai*, the opening *a* lines of the *lai nouveau* form a refrain for later stanzas alternately as in the VILLANELLE. The A^1 line closes stanza II; A^2 closes stanza III, and so on to the last stanza, where they are united in a couplet, *in reverse order*, to close the poem: A^{2}A^1. Though the *main* rhyme is usually carried from stanza to stanza, sometimes the short-line rhymes vary from stanza to stanza.

The schematic for a strict poem consisting of four eight-line stanzas would be plotted thus:

lines:	syllables, rhymes, refrains:
1.	x x x x A^1—*refrain*
2.	x x x x A^2—*refrain*
3.	x b
4.	x x x x a
5.	x x x x a

```
 6.     x  b
 7.     x  x  x  x  a
 8.     x  x  x  x  a

 9.     x  x  x  x  a
10.     x  x  x  x  a
11.     x  b
12.     x  x  x  x  a
13.     x  x  x  x  a
14.     x  b
15.     x  x  x  x  a
16.     x  x  x  x  A¹—refrain

17.     x  x  x  x  a
18.     x  x  x  x  a
19.     x  b
20.     x  x  x  x  a
21.     x  x  x  x  a
22.     x  b
23.     x  x  x  x  a
24.     x  x  x  x  A²—refrain

25.     x  x  x  x  a
26.     x  x  x  x  a
27.     x  b
28.     x  x  x  x  a
29.     x  x  x  x  a
30.     x  b
31.     x  x  x  x  A²—refrain
32.     x  x  x  x  A¹—refrain
```

The VIRELAI, like its sister forms, is a syllabic French stanza pattern. Its syllabic count is the same as the *lai*, and it has, as a rule, nine lines to the stanza, as does the *lai*. The difference is that the *long* lines of a following stanza pick up the short-line rhymes of the preceding stanza. This may be carried on indefinitely until the final stanza picks up as its short-line rhyme the long-line rhyme of the *first* stanza.

This is the pattern for a *virelai* of three stanzas:

lines:	syllables and rhymes:
1.	x x x x a
2.	x x x x a
3.	x b
4.	x x x x a
5.	x x x x a
6.	x b
7.	x x x x a
8.	x x x x a
9.	x b
10.	x x x x b
11.	x x x x b
12.	x c
13.	x x x x b
14.	x x x x b
15.	x c
16.	x x x x b
17.	x x x x b
18.	x c
19.	x x x x c
20.	x x x x c
21.	x a
22.	x x x x c
23.	x x x x c
24.	x a
25.	x x x x c
26.	x x x x c
27.	x a

For other forms that utilize this kind of interlocking rhyme see the interlocking RUBAIYAT, TERZA RIMA, and the TER-ZANELLE.

The LAI forms are strict, and should be distinguished from the LAY, which is not. See the section on LYRICS.

French. Originally syllabic but, in English, accentual-syllabic. A single QUINTET rhyming *aabba* and written in anapestic measures. Lines one, two, and five are of three anapestic feet; lines three and four contain two anapestic feet. Line five *may* be merely a modified repetition of line one.

lines:	*meters and rhymes:*		
1.	xxx́	xxx́	xxá
2.	xxx́	xxx́	xxá
3.	xxx́	xxb́	
4.	xxx́	xxb́	
5.	xxx́	xxx́	xxá

A related *stanza* form is the English MADSONG STANZA. Its rhyme scheme is $a^3b^3c^2c^2b^3$, its meters, susceptible to considerable variation, are usually iambic, trochaic, or dipodic, and the long lines often end either in spondees or with an extra unaccented syllable (i.e., the long lines often utilize feminine endings). See also *dipodics* and *sprung rhythm*.

The limerick is a form used primarily as a vehicle for nonsense verse. Like the EPIGRAM, it often turns on wit or word-play. The madsong is traditionally utilized as its name indicates—it is a *lyric* sung by a fool or madman.

A number of loose verse forms exist that have traditionally been used in certain lyric, or songlike contexts:

The ALBA or AUBADE is a love lyric that has *dawn* as its setting or subject.

ANACREONTICS are songs in praise of wine, women, and song. The meter is often trochaic tetrameter.

The CANSO or CANZO or CANZONE is a song about love and/or beauty.

A CANTICLE is a song derived from liturgy.

The CAROL is a joyous hymn; there is also a set form.

The CHANT is a work song or religious recitative that utilizes a *refrain*. See the CHANT ROYAL for a set form.

A CHANTEY is a sailor's work song.

The DITHYRAMB is a frenzied and raucous hymn in honor of revelry.

The ELEGY is a reflection upon *death* or some other equally serious subject. The DIRGE, THRENODY, or MONODY are similar, but are usually more intense songs of lamentation.

The EPITHALAMION is a lyric written in honor of a *wedding*. A *meditative* lyric upon the same subject is a PROTHALAMION.

The LAY is a short narrative song that is usually written in four-beat couplets. It is *not* to be confused with the French LAI, which is a set form.

The MADRIGAL is a lyric, usually about love, to be set to music. There is also a set form.

MADSONG (see the LIMERICK).

A NURSERY RHYME is any song, jingle, nonsense verse, or doggerel that is traditionally used for the entertainment of children. See also *dipodics* and *sprung rhythm*.

The ODE is a lyric, often occasional, written on a level, and in a tone of exaltation. There are set forms.

PALINODE (listed separately).

The PASTORAL or IDYL is a poem ostensibly about or set in the countryside, usually with shepherds or other rural types of people as the prime figures. However, it is often concerned with matters of more general or graver import.

The ECLOGUE is a pastoral cast in the form of a dialogue (see DRAMATICS). The PASTORAL ELEGY is a combination of the two lyric forms.

RIDDLE (see DIDACTICS).

The ROMANCE (or METRICAL ROMANCE, to distinguish it from prose) is a verse tale whose subject matter concerns *chivalry* or *honor*.

A ROUNDELAY is any simple lyric that utilizes a refrain. See RONDELET.

The RUNE is a poem of *incantation* or magic. It is often an ACROSTIC or an anagram.

The SERENADE is similar to the ALDA except that its setting is the *evening*.

The SIRVENTE is a lyric *satire* on either public matters or religion.

MADRIGAL

Italian and English. Accentual-syllabic. Written in lines of either seven or eleven syllables, the madrigal is comprised of two *or* three triplets, followed by one *or* two rhyming couplets. There is no set rhyme scheme for the triplets, but if the poem were written in TERZA RIMA it might look like this:

lines:	*rhymes:*
1.	a
2.	b
3.	a
4.	b
5.	c
6.	b
7.	c
8.	d
9.	c
10.	d
11.	d
12.	a
13.	a

For freer forms, see the section concerning LYRICS.

MOTE

Spanish. A mote is any poem complete in one or two lines, containing a complete statement or thought. The mote may serve as a *texte* to be glossed in verse (as a quatrain is glossed in the GLOSE).

There are any number of set single-line forms that might serve as motes, including the ALEXANDRINE, SEPTENARY, and the CLASSICAL HEROIC LINE.

See also the COUPLET.

OCTAVE

A *stanza* consisting of eight lines. It may be written in any meter, rhymed or unrhymed. Lines may be of any length. Rhymes, if any, may be random or regular.

The ITALIAN OCTAVE is written in iambic pentameter lines, and it rhymes *abbaabba* (see the Italian SONNET).

The SICILIAN OCTAVE is accentual-syllabic also. It is a *stanza* of iambic pentameter lines turning on two rhymes. It may also be a complete poem.

The diagram for the Sicilian octave:

lines:	meters and rhymes:				
1.	xx́	xx́	xx́	xx́	xá
2.	xx́	xx́	xx́	xx́	xb́
3.	xx́	xx́	xx́	xx́	xá
4.	xx́	xx́	xx́	xx́	xb́
5.	xx́	xx́	xx́	xx́	xá
6.	xx́	xx́	xx́	xx́	xb́
7.	xx́	xx́	xx́	xx́	xá
8.	xx́	xx́	xx́	xx́	xb́

The STRAMBOTTO is a Sicilian octave in hendecasyllabic lines.

For closely related forms see the Italian OCTAVE above, OTTAVA RIMA, the Sicilian SESTET, and the second ending of the Italian SONNET. See also the remarks concerning the HEROIC OCTAVE in the section dealing with the RISPETTO.

ODE

There are three more or less strict forms of the ode. The first is the PINDARIC ODE, which is of Greek origin. It is usually written in accentual-syllabic verse. The stanza pattern, rhyme scheme, and line lengths are determined by the poet.

The poem is divided into three *movements*, not necessarily stanzas. The *first movement*, called the *strophe*, and the *second movement*, called the *antistrophe*, are identical and strict in form, though the exact form is devised by the poet.

The *third* and last movement of the poem is called the *stand* or *epode*. Its form is strict also, but entirely different from that of the first two movements.

The ENGLISH ODE (or Keatsian ode) is accentual-syllabic. It consists of three ten-line iambic pentameter stanzas. Stanza one rhymes *ababcdecde:* stanzas two and three have the same scheme but their own rhymes.

The pattern for one stanza of the English ode:

lines:	meters and rhymes:				
1.	xx́	xx́	xx́	xx́	xá
2.	xx́	xx́	xx́	xx́	xb́
3.	xx́	xx́	xx́	xx́	xá
4.	xx́	xx́	xx́	xx́	xb́
5.	xx́	xx́	xx́	xx́	xć
6.	xx́	xx́	xx́	xx́	xd̂
7.	xx́	xx́	xx́	xx́	xé
8.	xx́	xx́	xx́	xx́	xć
9.	xx́	xx́	xx́	xx́	xd̂
10.	xx́	xx́	xx́	xx́	xé

The stanza pattern for the English ode was derived by combining elements of the English and Italian SONNET forms: a Sicilian QUATRAIN from the English sonnet (*abab*) is attached to an Italian SESTET (*cdecde*).

The HOMOSTROPHIC ODE (or Horatian ode) consists of any number of *formal* stanzas. However, the form of the stanzas is determined by the poet.

A fourth type, the Cowleyan or IRREGULAR ODE is a loose form, and it may be described simply as a serious LYRIC. Its structure, too, is determined by the poet.

A RONSARDIAN ODE is, strictly speaking, a *stanza form*. Such an ode may be of any length, provided each stanza is nine lines long, rhymes *ababccddc*, and varies its line-lengths between pentameter and dimeter iambic lines, in a specific order. The *last* line is a *tetrameter* line:

lines:	meters and rhymes:				
1.	xx́	xx́	xx́	xx́	xá
2.	xx́	xb́			
3.	xx́	xx́	xx́	xx́	xá
4.	xx́	xb́			
5.	xx́	xx́	xx́	xx́	xć
6.	xx́	xx́	xx́	xx́	xć
7.	xx́	xd̂			
8.	xx́	xd̂			
9.	xx́	xx́	xx́	xć	

An Italian *stanza* pattern. It may also be a complete poem. It is an OCTAVE stanza in iambic pentameter lines rhyming *abababcc*.

The scheme:

lines:	meters and rhymes:				
1.	xx́	xx́	xx́	xx́	xá
2.	xx́	xx́	xx́	xx́	xb́
3.	xx́	xx́	xx́	xx́	xá
4.	xx́	xx́	xx́	xx́	xb́
5.	xx́	xx́	xx́	xx́	xá
6.	xx́	xx́	xx́	xx́	xb́
7.	xx́	xx́	xx́	xx́	xć
8.	xx́	xx́	xx́	xx́	xć

Essentially, *ottava rima* is a Sicilian SESTET expanded by the addition of a HEROIC COUPLET.

For related forms see the Italian OCTAVE and the Sicilian OCTAVE. See also the remarks concerning the HEROIC OCTAVE in the section on the RISPETTO.

PALINODE

A Greek and Italian form. A palinode is a lyric, a "song of retraction" for a derogatory statement that has been made. A set form consists of *two strophes* and *two antistrophes*. These are of no traditional pattern but, as in the ODE, the poet sets a pattern that must be adhered to throughout the poem.

The pattern of the first strophe is mirrored in the last antistrophe; the pattern of the second strophe is mirrored in the first antistrophe, thus: strophe *A*, strophe *B*, antistrophe *B*, antistrophe *A*, in that order. The two strophes may be the statement, and the two antistrophes may be the retraction.

Technically, the two (differing) strophes are called the *ode*, and the two (differing) antistrophes are the "palinode" proper.

PANTOUM

A Malayan form. Accentual-syllabic. Lines may be of any length in any meter. A *pantoum* consists of an indefinite number of QUATRAIN stanzas with particular restrictions: lines two and four of each stanza, *in their entirety*, become lines one and three of the following stanza, and so on. These carry-over lines are called *repetons*. The rhyme scheme is *abab*, *bcbc*, etcetera.

The poem may be ended in one of two ways: either in a QUATRAIN whose repetons are lines one and three of the *first* stanza *in reversed order*; or the poem may end in a repeton couplet consisting of lines one and three of the first stanza *in reversed order*.

The pattern for a four-stanza poem:

lines:	*rhymes and repetons:*
1.	A^1
2.	B^1
3.	A^2
4.	B^2
5.	B^1
6.	C^1
7.	B^2
8.	C^2
9.	C^1
10.	D^1
11.	C^2
12.	D^2
13.	Z^1 *or* A^2
14.	A^2 A^1
15.	Z^2
16.	A^1

For another form that uses repetons, see the TERZANELLE.

PEARLINE STANZA

English. Accentual or accentual-syllabic. A twelve-line stanza written either with four *accents* to the line or in tetrameters. Alliteration, if written in accentual verse, as in ANGLO-SAXON PROSODY. The stanza turns on three rhymes and line *twelve* is a variable *refrain* that is carried through *two or more* stanzas. The *last word or phrase*, however, is constant for as long as the refrain is carried. The rhyme scheme is *ababababbcbC*.

A possible pattern for one stanza in accentuals:

lines:	words, syllables, alliterations, accents, caesuras, rhymes, refrains:
1.	ó óx · x óx xá
2.	x px́ px́ · x ṕ x b́
3.	q́ x q́xx · x q́x á
4.	x ŕx x ŕx · x ŕx b́
5.	x ś x śx · x ś xá
6.	x t́ x t́ · x t́x b́
7.	xú xxxú · x x ú á
8.	x v́ x v́xx · x v́ b́
9.	xẃ x ẃ · x ẃ x b́
10.	x f́ x f́ · x f́ x ć
11.	x ýx x ýx · x ýxb́
12.	x x źx ź · xźx Ĉ—*refrain*
13.	etcetera.

For further information concerning the Pearline stanza, see *sprung rhythm*.

POULTER'S MEASURE

English. Accentual-syllabic. Rhymed. A COUPLET that alternates the ALEXANDRINE (see also SPENSERIAN STANZA) and the *septenary* or FOURTEENER. There may be any number of couplets in a stanza or poem.

The Alexandrine is a LINE of iambic hexameter verse:

xx́ xx́ xx́ xx́ xx́ xx́.

The fourteener was, in Latin verse, a LINE consisting of seven metrical feet. In English verse the line contains fourteen syllables arranged in iambics, with a caesura appearing somewhere in the center of the line:

xx́ xx́ xx́ xx́ · xx́ xx́ xx́

A schematic of one couplet of Poulter's measure:

lines: *meters, caesuras, and rhymes:*

1.   xx́ xx́ xx́ xx́ xx́ xá
2.   xx́ xx́ xx́ xx́ · xx́ xx́ xá

QUATRAIN

A stanza or poem consisting of four lines. It may be written in any meter and line-length, and it may be rhymed or unrhymed.

The ENVELOPE STANZA is a quatrain stanza that rhymes *abba*. The so-called IN MEMORIAM STANZA is an iambic tetrameter envelope.

The REDONDILLA, a Spanish form of the envelope stanza, is an *octosyllabic* quatrain rhyming *abba*.

The ITALIAN QUATRAIN is an envelope stanza that is written in iambic pentameter measures:

lines:	*meters and rhymes:*				
1.	xx́	xx́	xx́	xx́	xá
2.	xx́	xx́	xx́	xx́	xb́
3.	xx́	xx́	xx́	xx́	xb́
4.	xx́	xx́	xx́	xx́	xá

Doubled, it becomes the ITALIAN OCTAVE, which is utilized in the Italian SONNET. The Italian quatrain is a form of HEROIC STANZA.

The SICILIAN QUATRAIN is also a set form of the HEROIC STANZA, and is the pattern for the quatrains found in the ENGLISH SONNET. It is the same as the Italian octave, except that it rhymes *abab*. Doubled, it becomes the Sicilian OCTAVE.

For other set forms and uses of the quatrain see the sections on AE FREISLIGHE, ALCAICS, AWDL GYWYDD, BALLAD STANZA, BYR A THODDAID, CASBAIRDNE, COMMON MEASURE, DEIBHIDHE, the ENGLYNS, GWAWDODYN, KYRIELLE, PANTOUM, the RANNAIGHEACHTS, RIONNAIRD TRI N-ARD, RISPETTO, ROUNDEL, RUBAI, SAPPHICS, SÉADNA, SNEADHBHAIRDNE, and TODDAID.

QUINTET

A poem or stanza consisting of five lines. It may be in any meter and line-length, rhymed or unrhymed.

The SICILIAN QUINTET is written in iambic pentameter measures, and it rhymes *ababa*.

The pattern:

lines:	meters and rhymes:				
1.	xx́	xx́	xx́	xx́	xá
2.	xx́	xx́	xx́	xx́	xb́
3.	xx́	xx́	xx́	xx́	xá
4.	xx́	xx́	xx́	xx́	xb́
5.	xx́	xx́	xx́	xx́	xá

The QUINTILLA, a Spanish form, is any *octosyllabic* quintet rhyming *ababa*, *abbab*, *abaab*, *aabab*, or *aabba*.

For other set forms of the quintet see the sections on the CINQUAIN, LIMERICK, and TANKA.

RANNAIGHEACHTS

Irish. Syllabic.

RANNAIGHEACHT GHAIRID is a QUATRAIN *stanza*. The first line is three syllables long, the rest are seven syllables in length. The quatrain single-rhymes *aaba*. Line *three* cross-rhymes with line *four*.

In *all* the Irish forms in this section and elsewhere, the *poem* (not the stanza) ends with the same first syllable, word, or line with which it begins.

The diagram for one stanza:

lines:	syllables and rhymes:
1.	x x a
2.	x x x x x x a
3.	x x x x x x b
4.	x *x* *b* x *x* x a
5.	etcetera.

When the lines in this form end in *disyllables* instead of monosyllables, it is called RANDAIGECHT CHETHARCHUBAID GARIT RÉCOMARCACH.

RANNAIGHEACHT MHÓR is a QUATRAIN *stanza* of seven-syllable lines *consonating*, not rhyming, *abab*. There are at least two cross-rhymes in each couplet, and the final word of line *three* rhymes with a word in the interior of line *four*. The internal rhyme in the first couplet may be slant-rhyme. In the *second* couplet the rhymes *must* be exact. Two words alliterate in each line, the final word of line *four* alliterating with the preceding stressed word.

A simplified schematic:

lines:	syllables, cross-rhymes, and consonates:	
1.	x x x x b x ac	—lines 1 and 3,
2.	x x x a x x bc	2 and 4 CONSO-
3.	x b x x x x ac	NATE, *not rhyme*
4.	x x a x x x bc	

Rannaigheacht bheag is the same, except the line endings are disyllabic.

Deachnadh mór is also the same, except that lines *one* and *three* are octosyllabic, lines *two* and *four* are hexasyllabic, and all line endings are disyllabic words.

RHUPUNT

Welsh. Syllabic. A LINE of three, four, *or* five sections. Each section contains four syllables. All but the last section rhyme with each other. The last section carries the *main* rhyme from line to line (or from stanza to stanza, depending on how the lines are set up: i.e., each section may be written on the page as a single line of verse).

In this pattern, each section is treated as one line, and each set of sections is treated as one stanza:

lines (or sections): *syllables and rhymes:*

1.	x	x	x	a
2.	x	x	x	a
3.	x	x	x	a
4.	x	x	x	B

—one line

5.	x	x	x	c
6.	x	x	x	c
7.	x	x	x	c
8.	x	x	x	B

—one line

9. etcetera.

After two lines (sets of sections) the main rhyme may change.

TAWDDGYRCH CADWYNOG is similarly a LINE of three, four, *or* five sections. Each section contains four syllables. The rhyme scheme is *abbc*. Each section must rhyme with its *corresponding* section in at least one other line of verse. If desired, each section may be written as one *line* of verse.

In the following schematic diagram each section is treated as one line, and each set of sections is treated as one stanza:

lines (or sections): *syllables and rhymes:*

1.	x	x	x	a
2.	x	x	x	b
3.	x	x	x	b
4.	x	x	x	c

—one line

```
5.              x   x   x   a⎫
6.              x   x   x   b⎪
7.              x   x   x   b⎬—one line
8.              x   x   x   c⎭

9.              etcetera.
```

After two lines (or sets of sections) the rhymes may change.

RIME COUÉE

French. Syllabic. A SESTET *stanza* made of two couplets of any length and two shorter lines. One of the short lines follows each couplet. The short lines rhyme with each other.

A schematic diagram of *rime couée* in iambics:

lines: *meters and rhymes*:
1.   xx́ xx́ xx́ xá
2.   xx́ xx́ xx́ xá
3.   xx́ xx́ xb́
4.   xx́ xx́ xx́ xć
5.   xx́ xx́ xx́ xć
6.   xx́ xx́ xb́

7.   etcetera.

The Scottish BURNS STANZA, or STANDARD HABBIE, a variation, rhymes $a^4a^4a^4b^2a^4b^2$.

For similar forms see the sections on the LAI and COMMON particular MEASURE.

RIME ROYAL

A Scottish form. Accentual-syllabic. A SEPTET *stanza* rhyming *ababbcc*. The lines are written in iambic pentameter measures.

Diagram:

lines: *meters and rhymes:*
1.   xx́ xx́ xx́ xx́ xá
2.   xx́ xx́ xx́ xx́ xb́
3.   xx́ xx́ xx́ xx́ xá
4.   xx́ xx́ xx́ xx́ xb́
5.   xx́ xx́ xx́ xx́ xb́
6.   xx́ xx́ xx́ xx́ xć
7.   xx́ xx́ xx́ xx́ xć

8.   etcetera.

Irish. Syllabic. A QUATRAIN *stanza* of hexasyllabic lines with disyllabic endings. Lines *two* and *four* rhyme, and line *three* consonates with them. There are two cross-rhymes in the second couplet, none in the first. There is alliteration in each line, and the last syllable of line *one* alliterates with the first accented word of line *two*. There are two cross-rhymes in the second couplet, none in the first.

The *poem* (not the stanza) ends with the same first syllable, word, or line with which it begins.

lines:	syllables and rhymes:
1.	x x x x <u>x a</u>
2.	x x x x <u>x bc</u>
3.	x b x x <u>x c</u> } —*line 3* CONSONATES *with*
4.	x x c x <u>x bc</u> } *2 and 4*
5.	etcetera.

RISPETTO

An Italian form. Accentual-syllabic. Any complete poem consisting of two rhyming QUATRAINS. Strict versions combine a Sicilian QUATRAIN and an Italian QUATRAIN. Another version has the *rispetto* rhyming *abab ccdd*. Many *rispettos* are written in iambic tetrameter measures:

lines:	meters and rhymes:			
1.	xx́	xx́	xx́	xá
2.	xx́	xx́	xx́	xb́
3.	xx́	xx́	xx́	xá
4.	xx́	xx́	xx́	xb́
5.	xx́	xx́	xx́	xć
6.	xx́	xx́	xx́	xć
7.	xx́	xx́	xx́	xd́
8.	xx́	xx́	xx́	xd́

If the *rispetto* is written in iambic pentameter, it will be seen that it can combine heroic forms—the Sicilian and Italian quatrains, or a Sicilian quatrain and two heroic couplets. It is thus a HEROIC RISPETTO.

The RISPETTO STANZA rhmes *abababcc*. If it is written in iambic pentameter it is a HEROIC OCTAVE.

A SONETTO RISPETTO combines one heroic octave with either an Italian or Sicilian SESTET.

RONDEAU

French. Syllabic. Lines may be of any length. Fifteen lines divided into three stanzas: one QUINTET, one QUATRAIN, and one SESTET. The poem turns on two rhymes and is built on one *refrain*. The refrain consists of *the first few words of the first line*.

In this pattern the refrain is represented by the letter *R*:

lines:	rhymes and refrains:	
1.	. . . R	a—*first line* CONTAINS *refrain*
2.		a
3.		b
4.		b
5.		a
6.		a
7.		a
8.		b
9.	. . . R	
10.		a
11.		a
12.		b
13.		b
14.		a
15.	. . . R	

The RONDEAU PRIME consists of twelve lines divided into two stanzas that rhyme *RabbaabR abbaR*. The *refrain* is the *first word of the first line;* it reappears as line seven and again as line twelve, ending the poem.

The pattern of the *rondeau prime:*

lines:	rhymes and refrains:	
1.	. . . R	a—*refrain is the first word*
2.		b
3.		b
4.		a
5.		a

| 6. | b |
| 7. | . . . R —*refrain* |

8.	a
9.	b
10.	b
11.	a
12.	. . . R —*refrain*

The RONDEAU REDOUBLÉ consists of twenty-five lines divided into five QUATRAINS and one QUINTET. Stanza one rhymes $RA^1B^1A^2B^2$; each line in this first quatrain, which is called the *texte*, is a refrain. A *fifth refrain* consists of the *first phrase of the first line*. Thus, in all, the texte contains five refrains.

The first phrase of line one (represented by the letter R) reappears as the unrhymed line twenty-five, which ends the poem; the entire first line of the poem (A^1) reappears as line eight, ending the second stanza; line two (B^1) reappears as line twelve, ending the third stanza; line three (A^2) reappears as line sixteen, ending the fourth stanza; line four (B^2) reappears as line twenty, ending the fifth stanza.

The diagram:

	lines:	*rhymes and refrains:*
	1.	. . . R A^1—1*st line* CONTAINS *a refrain and* IS *one*
Texte—	2.	B^1—*refrain*
	3.	A^2—*refrain*
	4.	B^2—*refrain*
	5.	b
	6.	a
	7.	b
	8.	A^1—*refrain*
	9.	a
	10.	b
	11.	a
	12.	B^1—*refrain*

13.	b
14.	a
15.	b
16.	A²—*refrain*
17.	a
18.	b
19.	a
20.	B²—*refrain*
21.	b
22.	a
23.	b
24.	a
25.	. . . R

For a similar form, see the GLOSE, also the SONNET RE-DOUBLÉ and the CAROL.

RONDEL

French. Syllabic. Thirteen lines of any length divided into three stanzas: two QUATRAINS and one QUINTET. The poem turns on two rhymes and is built on a two-line refrain. The first line reappears as line seven, and as line thirteen, which ends the poem. The second line reappears as line eight, which ends the second stanza.

The schematic diagram:

lines:	rhymes and refrains:
1.	A—*refrain*
2.	B—*refrain*
3.	b
4.	a
5.	a
6.	b
7.	A
8.	B
9.	a
10.	b
11.	b
12.	a
13.	A—*refrain*

The RONDEL PRIME is one line longer. The double refrain forms lines thirteen and fourteen; thus, the last stanza would be a SESTET instead of a quintet, and the scheme would look like this:

9.	a
10.	b
11.	b
12.	a
13.	A—*refrain*
14.	B—*refrain*

RONDELET

French. Syllabic. A SEPTET *poem*. The *first* line is a refrain, which reappears as lines three and seven. The refrain is four syllables in length. The rest of the lines (two, four, five, and six) are eight syllables in length. Line four rhymes with the refrain. Lines two, five, and six have their own rhyme.
  Scheme:

lines:	syllables, rhymes, and refrains:
1.	x x x A
2.	x x x x x x x b
3.	x x x A
4.	x x x x x x x a
5.	x x x x x x x b
6.	x x x x x x x b
7.	x x x A

See ROUNDELAY among the LYRICS.

ROUNDEL

An English form. Accentual-syllabic. Lines may be of any length. Eleven lines broken into three stanzas: a QUATRAIN, a TRIPLET, and a QUATRAIN, in that order. The poem turns on two rhymes and is built on one *refrain*. The refrain consists of the *first word or group of words* in the first line. The refrain (*R*) *rhymes internally* with the *last word of the second line*. Short scheme: $R^b abaR^b \, bab \, abaR^b$.

The diagram:

lines:	rhymes and refrain:	
1.	R^b	a—*1st line contains rhyming refrain*
2.		b
3.		a
4.	R^b	—*refrain*
5.		b
6.		a
7.		b
8.		a
9.		b
10.		a
11.	R^b	—*refrain*

Arabic. Accentual-syllabic. A complete poem consisting of one QUATRAIN rhyming *aaba*. Lines are often tetrameter or pentameter, and all are of the same length:

lines:	meters and rhymes:
1.	xx́ xx́ xx́ xá
2.	xx́ xx́ xx́ xá
3.	xx́ xx́ xx́ xb́
4.	xx́ xx́ xx́ xá

A RUBAIYAT is a poem composed of a number of these quatrains utilized as stanzas.

In the INTERLOCKING RUBAIYAT the end-sound of line *three* in the first stanza becomes the rhyme in the second stanza; the same is true for succeeding stanzas, each of which picks up its rhyme from the third line of the preceding stanza. In the *last* stanza the third line takes its end-sound from the rhyme of the first stanza.

The diagram for a four-stanza poem:

lines:	rhymes:
1.	a
2.	a
3.	b
4.	a
5.	b
6.	b
7.	c
8.	b
9.	c
10.	c
11.	d
12.	c

13.   d
14.   d
15.   a
16.   d

For other forms that use interlocking rhyme see TERZA RIMA and the TERZANELLE.

SAPPHICS

A Greek form. Accentual-syllabic. Unrhymed. In English meters, a SAPPHIC LINE consists of eleven syllables and five verse feet, the central foot being a dactyl; the other four feet, two on either side of the central dactyl, are trochees.

A SAPPHIC STANZA is composed of three such lines plus one that is shorter, called an ADONIC: one dactyl followed by one trochee.

The rhythms of each line are *falling rhythms*: the accents of all verse feet fall on the *first* syllable—the endings of the lines are consequently *feminine endings*. The opposite of this, in which the accents fall on the last syllable of all verse feet, is called *rising rhythm*, and the line endings would be *masculine*.

There may be any number of stanzas in a Sapphic poem: the stanzas are QUATRAINS.

A spondee *may* be substituted for a trochee in lines one and two, feet two and five; and in line three, foot five—see the *italicized* sections of the diagram:

lines:	*meters:*				
1.	x́x	*x́x*	x́xx	x́x	*x́x*
2.	x́x	*x́x*	x́xx	x́x	*x́x*
3.	x́x	x́x	x́xx	x́x	*x́x*
4.	x́xx	x́x			

SATIRICS

There are three forms that are often used in a satirical context.

The EPIGRAM is accentual-syllabic as a rule. It is a brief, usually rhymed poem on a single idea with an inversion or shift in thought that focuses on wit, satire, or some other intellectual gambit. It is perhaps better described as terse verse with a cutting edge. Epigrams have no set form, though they are often quatrains or couplets.

The EPITAPH is similar except that it is (ostensibly) an inscription for a tomb. The literary epitaph, like the epigram, often focuses on wit or satire and might be described as terse verse for the long gone.

SKELTONICS are short, usually dipodic or tripodic (two–foot or three-foot) *lines*, insistently and humorously rhymed, utilizing heavily accented rhythms and alliteration for satiric effect. Skeltonics are sometimes called *tumbling verse*. See also *dipodics* and *sprung rhythm*.

HUDIBRASTICS are irregular octosyllabic or tetrametric lines, humorously rhymed in couplets.

Another satiric line is the NASHER, which will be found in the section dealing with FREE VERSE.

The FABLIAU, a French form, is a short verse narrative, usually in octosyllabic couplets (see HUDIBRASTICS, above, and CYHYDEDD FER), that takes its material from the middle classes.

Such forms as Skeltonics, Hudibrastics, and Nashers are modes of DOGGEREL verse. Generally speaking, doggerel is any irregularly structured verse broad in its comic effect and aimed primarily at caricature and burlesque.

Any form may be used satirically. When this occurs, the word *mock* is usually prefixed to the name of the form, as in "mock-epic," "mock-ode," and so forth.

SÉADNA

Irish. Syllabic. A QUATRAIN stanza of alternating octo-syllabic lines with disyllabic endings, and heptasyllabic lines with monosyllabic endings. Lines *two* and *four* rhyme; line *three* rhymes with the stressed word preceding the final word of line *four*. There are two cross-rhymes in the second couplet. There is alliteration in each line, the final word of line *four* alliterating with the preceding stressed word. The final syllable of line *one* alliterates with the first stressed word of line *two*.

The *poem* (not the stanza) ends with the same first syllable, word, or line with which it begins.

A simplified version:

lines:	syllables and rhymes:
1.	x x x x x x <u>x</u> a
2.	x x x x x x <u>b</u>
3.	x x x *x* c *x* <u>x c</u>
4.	x b x c x x <u>b</u>

SÉADNA MÓR is the same except that lines *two* and *four* have trisyllabic endings.

SEPTET

A stanza *or* poem consisting of seven lines in any meter, rhymed or unrhymed.

The SICILIAN SEPTET is written in iambic pentameter measures rhyming *abababa:*

lines:	meters and rhymes:
1.	xx́ xx́ xx́ xx́ xá
2.	xx́ xx́ xx́ xx́ xb́
3.	xx́ xx́ xx́ xx́ xá
4.	xx́ xx́ xx́ xx́ xb́
5.	xx́ xx́ xx́ xx́ xá
6.	xx́ xx́ xx́ xx́ xb́
7.	xx́ xx́ xx́ xx́ xá

For other set forms and uses of the septet see the sections on RIME ROYAL and the RONDELET.

SESTET

A stanza *or* poem consisting of six lines in any meter, rhymed or unrhymed.

The ITALIAN SESTET is written in iambic pentameter measures, and it rhymes *abcabc*.

The SICILIAN SESTET is the same, but it rhymes *ababab*:

lines:	meters and rhymes:
1.	xx́ xx́ xx́ xx́ xá
2.	xx́ xx́ xx́ xx́ xb́
3.	xx́ xx́ xx́ xx́ xá
4.	xx́ xx́ xx́ xx́ xb́
5.	xx́ xx́ xx́ xx́ xá
6.	xx́ xx́ xx́ xx́ xb́

A HEROIC SESTET is written in iambic pentameter measures and rhymes *ababcc*.

The SEXTILLA, a Spanish form, is an *octosyllablic* sestet rhyming either *aabccb* or *ababcc*.

A sestet that utilizes the BOB (see BOB AND WHEEL) is the Scottish BURNS STANZA or STANDARD HABBIE (see RIME COUÉE).

For various uses and relatives of these forms see the SICILIAN OCTAVE, OTTAVA RIMA, ITALIAN SONNET, and SONETTO RISPETTO.

SESTINA

French. Syllabic. Thirty-nine lines divided into six SESTETS and one TRIPLET, which is called the *envoy*. The poem is ordinarily unrhymed. Instead of rhymes, the six *end-words* of the lines in stanza one are picked up and re-used *in a particular order*, as end-words in the remaining stanzas. In the envoy, which ends the poem, the six end-words are also picked up: *one* end-word is buried in each line, and *one* end-word finishes each line. Lines may be of any length.

The order in which the end-words are re-used is prescribed by a set pattern as follows:

lines:	repeated end-words:
1.	A
2.	B
3.	C
4.	D
5.	E
6.	F
7.	F
8.	A
9.	E
10.	B
11.	D
12.	C
13.	C
14.	F
15.	D
16.	A
17.	B
18.	E
19.	E
20.	C
21.	B

22.	F	
23.	A	
24.	D	
25.	D	
26.	E	
27.	A	
28.	C	
29.	F	
30.	B	
31.	B	
32.	D	
33.	F	
34.	E	
35.	C	
36.	A	
37.	B	E
38.	D	C *—envoy*
39.	F	A

The rationale behind the sequence of recurring end-words seems to lie in the numerological sequence of numbers 615243. If this set of numbers is applied to *each* stanza's set of end-words, it will be seen that preceding end-words appear in the succeeding stanza in this order. Thus, apply the set of numbers, for instance to stanza two:

stanza 2:	*numbers:*	*equals stanza 3:*
F	6	C
A	1	F
E	5	D
B	2	A
D	4	B
C	3	E

What the numerological significance of the set is, however, has evidently been lost since the Middle Ages, though the form is still a popular one.

SNEADHBHAIRDNE

Irish. Syllabic. A QUATRAIN *stanza* of alternating octo-syllabic and quadrasyllabic lines ending in disyllabic words. Lines *two* and *four* rhyme, line *three* consonates with them. Every stressed word in line *four* must rhyme. Alliteration as in RIONNAIRD TRI N-ARD.

The *poem* (not the stanza) ends with the same first syllable, word, or line with which it begins.

lines:	*syllables and rhymes:*
1.	x x x x x x x a
2.	x x x b
3.	x x x x x x x c
4.	b b x b

SONNET

Accentual-syllabic. Roughly speaking, any fourteen-line poem written in rhymed iambic pentameter verse. However, there are two basic traditional patterns of the sonnet.

The Petrarchan or ITALIAN SONNET is divided into an OCTAVE and a SESTET. The octave's rhyme is *abba abba* (see ITALIAN OCTAVE). The sestet's rhyme varies, but it is generally either *cde cde* (ITALIAN SESTET) or *cdcdcd* (SICILIAN SESTET):

lines:	meters and rhymes:									
1.	xx́	xx́	xx́	xx́	xá					
2.	xx́	xx́	xx́	xx́	xb́					
3.	xx́	xx́	xx́	xx́	xb́					
4.	xx́	xx́	xx́	xx́	xá					
5.	xx́	xx́	xx́	xx́	xá					
6.	xx́	xx́	xx́	xx́	xb́					
7.	xx́	xx́	xx́	xx́	xb́					
8.	xx́	xx́	xx́	xx́	xá					
9.	xx́	xx́	xx́	xx́	xć	*or*	xx́	xx́	xx́	xx́	xć
10.	xx́	xx́	xx́	xx́	xd́		xx́	xx́	xx́	xx́	xd́
11.	xx́	xx́	xx́	xx́	xé		xx́	xx́	xx́	xx́	xć
12.	xx́	xx́	xx́	xx́	xć		xx́	xx́	xx́	xx́	xd́
13.	xx́	xx́	xx́	xx́	xd́		xx́	xx́	xx́	xx́	xć
14.	xx́	xx́	xx́	xx́	xé		xx́	xx́	xx́	xx́	xd́

The Shakespearian or ENGLISH SONNET is divided into three SICILIAN QUATRAINS and one HEROIC COUPLET. It is written in iambic pentameter measures:

lines:	rhymes:
1.	a
2.	b
3.	a
4.	b
5.	c
6.	d

7.	c
8.	d
9.	e
10.	f
11.	e
12.	f
13.	g
14.	g

The CROWN OF SONNETS is a sequence of seven Italian sonnets. The *last line* of each of the first six sonnets becomes the first line of the ensuing sonnet; the last line of the seventh sonnet is the first line of the first sonnet. Since the seven sonnets are considered to be one poem, no rhyme sounds or words may be re-used except in the formally repeated lines.

The SONNET REDOUBLÉ is a chain of fifteen sonnets. *Each* of the fourteen lines in the *first* sonnet (called the *texte*) becomes, in order, the *final line* in the following fourteen sonnets. A variation of this pattern makes each of the lines in the texte the *first line* in the following fourteen sonnets. For other forms that use a *texte*, see the CAROL, the GLOSE, and the RONDEAU REDOUBLÉ.

The SPENSERIAN SONNET is a chain of three SICILIAN QUATRAINS, the second and third of which pick up their first-line rhymes from the last-line rhymes of the first and second quatrains respectively, plus a HEROIC COUPLET: *abab bcbc cdcd ee.*

The tailed or CAUDATED SONNET adds two three-foote tsail and two heroic couplets to the Italian sonnet ands rhym *abbaabba cdecde e³fff³gg*; thus, it is twenty lines long.

An eighteen-line form is the HEROIC SONNET, which adds a HEROIC COUPLET to two stanzas of HEROIC OCTAVE (see the section on the RISPETTO).

A SONNET SEQUENCE is a group of sonnets on a single subject.

For other fourteen-line forms (QUATORZAINS) see the BREF DOUBLE, the SONETTO RISPETTO and the TERZA RIMA sonnet.

SPATIALS

Variously called the CALLIGRAMME, the SHAPED STANZA, or HIEROGLYPHIC VERSE, spatials may be in any form or meter. What is of importance in spatial verse is *how the poem appears on paper*: it attempts to imitate typographically a particular shape, usually one discussed in the poem itself.

Concrete verse is ideogrammic spatials. For instance. in Japanese the characters for "rain" might be arranged on the page so that it will *look* like rain falling. At the bottom of the picture there might be the character for "house"; thus, the characters for rain are falling pictorially on the character for house.

In an alphabetical language such as English concrete verse is more difficult to write and not so immediately effective. The letters of a word must be *drawn* so as to imitate the subject; i.e., the letters in the word "murder" may be drawn so as to represent a dagger.

SPENSERIAN STANZA

English. Accentual-syllabic. A rhymed *stanza* of nine
lines consisting of eight iambic pentameter lines and one
iambic hexameter line, which is called an *Alexandrine*. The
Alexandrine is always the last (ninth) line of the stanza.
There is no set pattern for the rhymes.

A possible scheme:

lines:	meters and rhymes:				
1.	xx́	xx́	xx́	xx́	xá
2.	xx́	xx́	xx́	xx́	xb́
3.	xx́	xx́	xx́	xx́	xá
4.	xx́	xx́	xx́	xx́	xb́
5.	xx́	xx́	xx́	xx́	xb́
6.	xx́	xx́	xx́	xx́	xá
7.	xx́	xx́	xx́	xx́	xá
8.	xx́	xx́	xx́	xx́	xb́
9.	xx́	xx́	xx́	xx́	xx́ xá

For another use of the Alexandrine, see POULTER'S MEA-
SURE.

For a form of Spenserian stanza with a set rhyme scheme,
see the HUITAIN.

STAVE

English. Accentual-syllabic. Loosely, the *stanza* of a hymn or of a drinking song, both of which often utilize *refrains*. Usually, lines are tetrameter or shorter. The term may be applied more specifically to a *sestet* stanza made of three couplets and ending in a refrain: *aabbcC, ddeecC,* etc.

In a stricter version, both the first and last lines of each stave are the refrain. Thus, only the rhyme of the central couplet changes from stanza to stanza:

lines:	rhymes and refrains:
1.	A
2.	a
3.	b
4.	b
5.	a
6.	A
7.	A
8.	a
9.	c
10.	c
11.	a
12.	A
13.	etcetera.

The strict stave is a variation of the COUPLET ENVELOPE: two couplets rhyming *a* enclosing another rhyming couplet: *aabbaa.*

For other couplet forms see COUPLET, DIDACTICS, FREE VERSE, HEROICS, and POULTER'S MEASURE. For sestet forms see CLOGYRNACH, CYWYDD LLOSGYRNOG, GWAWDODYN HIR, HIR A THODDAID, RIME COUÉE, SESTET, and SHORT PARTICULAR MEASURE. See also the ENVELOPE STANZA,

TANKA

A Japanese form. Syllabic. The tanka is a single QUINTET whose lines consist of five, seven, five, seven, and seven syllables respectively. It is unrhymed:

lines:	syllables:						
1.	x	x	x	x	x		
2.	x	x	x	x	x	x	x
3.	x	x	x	x	x		
4.	x	x	x	x	x	x	x
5.	x	x	x	x	x	x	x

Note that the tanka is merely a HAIKU (see TERCET) with two added lines of seven syllables each. For this reason, a separation is sometimes made between the third and fourth lines, making it a poem consisting of one TRIPLET and one COUPLET.

The idea behind a TANKA CHAIN is as follows: a haiku is written. A TANKA COUPLET is added, completing the tanka. Another haiku is added that follows logically, but that may also be read logically in place of the *first* haiku. A couplet is added completing the second tanka. A third haiku is added that may be read logically if substituted for the second haiku. A couplet is added completing the third tanka, and so on indefinitely.

TERCET

May be written in any of the meters. Any complete poem of three lines, rhymed or unrhymed.

The ENCLOSED TERCET rhymes *aba* (see enclosed TRIPLET).

The SICILIAN TERCET is an enclosed tercet written in iambic pentameter measures (see the Sicilian TRIPLET).

The TRIAD is a loose Irish form. However, a strict version consists of three tercets, each a complete poem, yet each bearing some relationship to the other two, and the whole also being interpretable as one poem. Like the other Irish forms, the triad *may* end with the first syllable, word, or line with which it began.

The *hokku* or HAIKU is a Japanese tercet. Its lines consist of five, seven, and five syllables respectively. It is unrhymed:

lines:	*syllables:*						
1.	x	x	x	x	x		
2.	x	x	x	x	x	x	x
3.	x	x	x	x	x		

For a form related to the *haiku* see the TANKA.

TERZA RIMA

Italian. Accentual-syllabic. Any number of interlocking enclosed TRIPLET *stanzas*. The *first* and *third* lines of a stanza rhyme; the *second* line rhymes with the *first* and *third* lines of the *following* stanza. In other words, the ending of the second line of any stanza becomes the rhyme for the following stanza: *aba bcb cdc*, etc. The *poem* usually ends in a COUPLET rhymed from the second line of the last triplet: *yzy zz*. The meter is usually iambic pentameter.

Pattern:

lines:	*meters and rhymes:*				
1.	xx́	xx́	xx́	xx́	xá
2.	xx́	xx́	xx́	xx́	xb́
3.	xx́	xx́	xx́	xx́	xá
4.	xx́	xx́	xx́	xx́	xb́
5.	xx́	xx́	xx́	xx́	xć
6.	xx́	xx́	xx́	xx́	xb́
7.	xx́	xx́	xx́	xx́	xć
8.	xx́	xx́	xx́	xx́	xd́
9.	xx́	xx́	xx́	xx́	xć
10.	xx́	xx́	xx́	xx́	xd́
11.	xx́	xx́	xx́	xx́	xd́

The TERZA RIMA SONNET is a fourteen-line QUATORZAIN in iambic pentameter rhyming *aba bcb cdc ded ee*.

For a related form see the TERZANELLE. Another interlocking form is the interlocking RUBAIYAT. See also the MADRIGAL.

124

TERZANELLE

French. Syllabic. Lines may be of any length. An adaptation of TERZA RIMA to the VILLANELLE form. Nineteen lines long, composed of five interlocking enclosed TRIPLETS and a final QUATRAIN. Lines *one* and *three* reappear as refrains in the final quatrain. In addition, the middle line of each triplet is a *repeton* that reappears as the final line of the succeeding triplet, except the middle line of the last triplet, which reappears in the quatrain.

The poem may end in one of two ways, as in the diagram:

lines:	rhymes, repetons, and refrains:
1.	A^1—*refrain*
2.	B
3.	A^2—*refrain*
4.	b
5.	C
6.	B
7.	c
8.	D
9.	C
10.	d
11.	E
12.	D
13.	e
14.	F
15.	E
16.	f
17.	A^1—*refrain* *or* F
18.	F A^1—*refrain*
19.	A^2—*refrain* A^2—*refrain*

For another form that utilizes the repeton, see the PANTOUM. Another interlocking form is the interlocking RUBAIYAT.

TODDAID

Welsh. Syllabic. QUATRAIN stanzas alternating between ten-syllable and nine-syllable lines. A syllable toward the end of the *first* line cross-rhymes into the middle of the *second*, and the same effect is reproduced in lines *three* and *four*. Lines *two* and *four* rhyme with each other.

The diagram:

lines:	syllables and rhymes:
1.	x x x x x x *a* *x* *x* *x*
2.	x x x *x* *a* x x x b
3.	x x x x x x *x* *x* *c* *x*
4.	x x x *c* *x* *x* x x b
5.	etcetera.

TRIOLET

A French form. Syllabic. A poem consisting of a single OCTAVE turning on two rhymes. It is built on two *refrains:* line one reappears complete as line four and again as line seven; line two reappears as line eight, completing the poem. The triolet rhymes *ABaAabAB*. Lines may be of any length.

The plot:

lines:	*refrains and rhymes:*
1.	A—*refrain*
2.	B—*refrain*
3.	a
4.	A—*refrain*
5.	a
6.	b
7.	A—*refrain*
8.	B—*refrain*

Sometimes a separation is made between lines five and six, making it a poem of two stanzas: a QUINTET and a TRIPLET.

TRIPLET

A *stanza* consisting of three lines. It may be written in any of the meters and may be rhymed or unrhymed.

The ENCLOSED TRIPLET rhymes *aba*.

The SICILIAN TRIPLET is an enclosed triplet in iambic pentameter measures:

lines:	meters and rhymes:				
1.	xx́	xx́	xx́	xx́	xá
2.	xx́	xx́	xx́	xx́	xb́
3.	xx́	xx́	xx́	xx́	xá
4.	etcetera.				

There are two Welsh ENGLYNS that are triplet stanza forms. Both are syllabic.

ENGLYN MILWR turns on one rhyme, and each line has a count of seven syllables:

lines:	syllables and rhymes:					
1.	x	x	x	x	x	x	a
2.	x	x	x	x	x	x	a
3.	x	x	x	x	x	x	a
4.	etcetera.					

ENGLYN PENFYR is a stanza whose lines consist respectively of ten, seven, and seven syllables rhyming *AAA*. One, two, *or* three syllables occur at the end of the *first* line *after* the *main* rhyme. These syllables are *echoed* by assonance, alliteration, *or* secondary rhyme in the *first few* syllables of the *second* line. The main rhyme *ends* the second and third lines:

lines:	syllables and rhymes:									
1.	x	x	x	x	x	x	x	x	x	A	b
2.	b	x	x	x	x	x	A			
3.	x	x	x	x	x	x	A			

4.	x	x	x	x	x	x	C	*x*	*x*	*d*
5.	*x*	*d*	*x*	x	x	x	C			
6.	x	x	x	x	x	x	C			
7.	x	x	x	x	x	x	x	E	*x*	*f*
8.	*f*	*x*	*x*	x	x	x	E			
9.	x	x	x	x	x	x	E			
10.	etcetera.									

For set forms and uses of the triplet or enclosed triplet also see the sections on the TERCET, TERZA RIMA, TERZA-NELLE, TRIVERSEN, and VILLANELLE.

TRIVERSEN

This is a native form. It, and variations of it, have been appearing in American verse with some regularity during the twentieth century, but it is here isolated and named for the first time.

It is written in either accentual or accentual-syllabic measures. The triversen is eighteen lines long and is composed of six *end-stopped* TRIPLETS. Each line equals approximately one phrase, and each triplet equals one clause. In each line there are generally *no more* than four and *no less* than two accented syllables. Otherwise, lines may be of any length. The poem may be rhymed or unrhymed.

In the case of the metrical version, read *verse feet* for "accented syllables."

A possible scheme in accentuals:

lines:	*words, accents, syllables, sentences:*
1.	x́ xx́ x xx́x xx x́
2.	xx́ xxx́ x x́
3.	xxx́ x x́x.—*end 1st sentence*
4.	etcetera for 18 lines: 6 end–stopped triplets, each of which is one sentence or clause.

A somewhat similar form is the TRIAD, which will be found in the section on the TERCET.

For an explanation of the general prosody (sometimes called "projective verse") behind the triversen, see *variable foot.*

VERSE NARRATIVES

Most forms may be utilized as vehicles for narration or *story-telling*. However, certain forms traditionally serve this function, particularly the BALLAD, EPIC, FABLIAU, LAY, and ROMANCE, all of which are dealt with elsewhere in this book. However, the three major forms might be ranked and defined thus:

    I.   EPIC: A long, heroic verse narrative.
    II. ROMANCE: A long, lyric verse narrative.
   III. BALLAD: A relatively short, lyric verse narrative.

The two minor forms might be defined, very loosely, in this way:

   IV. FABLIAU: A short-story in rhymed verse.
    V. LAY: A vignette in song form.

See the sections on the BALLAD and related forms. For further information about the epic, see the section concerned with HEROICS; for the lay and romance, see the LYRICS section; for the *fabliau*, see SATIRICS.

VILLANELLE

A French form. Syllabic. Lines may be of any length. Nineteen lines divided into six stanzas—five TRIPLETS and one QUATRAIN—turning on two rhymes and built on two refrains. The refrains consist of lines one and three complete. Line one reappears as lines six, twelve, and eighteen; line three reappears as lines nine, fifteen, and nineteen, finishing the poem. The rhyme scheme is A^1bA^2 abA^1 abA^2 abA^1 abA^2 abA^1A^2:

lines:	refrains and rhymes:
1.	A^1—*refrain*
2.	b
3.	A^2—*refrain*
4.	a
5.	b
6.	A^1—*refrain*
7.	a
8.	b
9.	A^2—*refrain*
10.	a
11.	b
12.	A^1—*refrain*
13.	a
14.	b
15.	A^2—*refrain*
16.	a
17.	b
18.	A^1—*refrain*
19.	A^2—*refrain*

Bibliography of Examples:

A List of Recommended *Contemporary* Poems
Written in the Various Forms,
and Variations of the Forms.

ACROSTIC: "Song Made in Lieu of Other Ornaments"
by Spencer Brown, in *Poets of Today III*, ed. Wheelock
(Charles Scribner's Sons, 1956); "Knife Is the Name:
To Write in Less than Blood," "Jacks and Jills Who
Find the Day's Eyes Gone" in *The Sorrows of Cold Stone*,
by John Malcolm Brinnin (Dodd, Mead and Co., 1951);
"Flights" in *The Lovemaker*, by Robert Mezey (Cumming-
ton Press, 1961).

ANGLO-SAXON PROSODY: "The Coming of Robin Hood,"
Section V of "A Little Geste" in *A Little Geste*, by Daniel
G. Hoffman (Oxford University Press, 1960).

BALLAD: "Dick Dongworth on the Death of Roseblush"
in *A Crackling of Thorns*, by John Hollander (Yale Uni-
versity Press, 1958); "The Ballad of Red Fox" in *The Clev-
er Body*, by Melvin Walker LaFollette (Spenserian Press,
1959); "The Good Man" in *Walls and Distances*, by David
Galler (The Macmillan Co., 1959); "An Immigrant
Ballad" in *First Poems*, by Lewis Turco (Golden Quill
Press, 1960).

BALLAD STANZA: "The Man in the Man-Made Moon" in
Nude Descending a Staircase, by X. J. Kennedy (Doubleday
& Co., 1961).

BALLADE: "Ballade of the Inventory: In Provence" in
Light and Dark, by Barbara Howes (Wesleyan University
Press, 1959); "Ballade for Braque" in *Coming of Age*, by
Babette Deutsch (Indiana University Press, 1959);
"Mother of the Saint" in *The Love Letters of Phyllis
McGinley* (Viking Press, 1954); "Ballade of Blind Alleys"

by Vassar Miller, in *The New Orleans Poetry Journal*, Vol. I, no. 4, 1955; "Ballade of the Session after Camillo," by David Galler, *Walls and Distances*, *op. cit.*

BLANK VERSE: "The Fishermen" in *Green with Beasts*, by W. S. Merwin (London: Rupert Hart-Davis, 1956); "A Gloomy Looking Man" in *The Pageless Air*, by Ralph L. Kinsey (Golden Quill Press, 1959); "The Death of Venus" in *The Death of Venus, and Others*, by Harold Witt (Golden Quill Press, 1958).

CHANT ROYAL: "The Old Professor," by Lewis Turco, *First Poems*, *op. cit.*

CINQUAIN: "The Soul" by Babette Deutsch, *Coming of Age*, *op. cit.*; "St. John, Baptist," "St. Sebastian," "St. Francis of Assisi" by Melvin Walker La Follette, *The Clever Body*, *op. cit.*

COMMON MEASURE: "Totentanz" by Lewis Turco, (untitled first poem in) *First Poems*, *op. cit.*

COUPLET: "The Wisdom of Insecurity" in *Great Praises*, by Richard Eberhart (Oxford University Press, 1957); "The Drunken Fisherman" in *Lord Weary's Castle*, by Robert Lowell (Harcourt, Brace, 1961).

CYHYDEDD FER: "Exclusive Blue" in *The Orb Weaver*, by Robert Francis (Wesleyan University Press, 1960); "Cormorants" in *Colonel Johnson's Ride*, by Robert Huff (Wayne State University Press, 1958); "The House and the Tree," by Spencer Brown, *Poets of Today III*, *op. cit.*

CYWYDD LLOSGYRNOG: "Where Once the Waters of Your Face" in *Collected Poems*, by Dylan Thomas (New Directions Books, 1953).

ENGLYNS and ALL OTHER WELSH FORMS: Various poems in *Green Armor on Green Ground*, by Rolfe Humphries (Charles Scribner's Sons, 1956).

ENGLYN UNODL CRWCA: "On a Wedding Anniversary" by Dylan Thomas, *Collected Poems*, *op. cit.*

EPIGRAM: "Palaver's No Prayer" in 39 *Poems*, by John Ciardi (Rutgers University Press, 1959); various poems in *The Exclusions of a Rhyme*, by J. V. Cunningham (Alan Swallow, 1960).

EPITAPH: "Epitaph for Our Landlord" in *Portrait of Your Niece*, by Carol Hall (University of Minnesota Press, 1959); "Epitaph" by Robert Francis, *The Orb Weaver*, *op. cit.*; "Little Elegy," "Epitaph for a Postal Clerk" by X. J. Kennedy, *Nude Descending a Staircase*, *op. cit.*

GLOSE: "Homage to J. S. Bach" in *The Crow and the Heart*, by Hayden Carruth (The Macmillan Co., 1959).

HAIKU: "Haiku: A Seasonal Sequence" by Clara M. Cassidy, in *Japan: Theme & Variations*, ed. Tuttle (Chas. E. Tuttle Co., 1959).

HENDECASYLLABICS: "Hendecasyllabics" by John Hollander, in *Fine Arts Magazine* (University of Connecticut), Vol. IV, no. 1, 1959.

HEROIC COUPLET: "It Is June, This Jesting Heat" by Robert Mezey, *The Lovemaker*, *op. cit.*; "Andromeda" by Graham Hough, in *Poetry 1960—An Appetiser*, a supplement of *The Critical Quarterly*, 1960.

KYRIELLE: "Sunday Psalm" by Phyllis McGinley, *The Love Letters*, *op. cit.*; "Dinky" in *Words for the Wind*, by Theodore Roethke (Doubleday & Co., 1958).

MADSONG: "Odds Bodkin's Springsong" by Lewis Turco in *Red Clay Reader 3*, 1966; "The Song of Mad Tom's Dog," in *Songs*, by Christopher Logue (McDowell-Obolensky, 1959).

NASHERS: Many poems by Ogden Nash in his various books.

OCTAVE: "Improvising" in *The World's One Clock*, by Louise Townsend Nicholl (St. Martin's Press, 1959); "Coffee-House Lecture" by Robert Mezey in *The Lovemaker*, *op. cit.*; "A Song for the Middle of the Night" in *The Green Wall*, by James Wright (Yale University Press, 1957).

ODE: "Summer: University Town" in *The Gazebos* by Edwin Honig (Clarke & Way, Inc., 1959); "Necromanteion" by Lewis Turco in *The Carolina Quarterly*, Vol. XVI, no. 1, 1963, and "Ode for the Beat Generation" by the same author in *First Poems*, *op. cit.*

OTTAVA RIMA: "Flag Day 1954," "The Spy to the Hero"

in *Last Poems*, by Edgar Bogardus (Kenyon Review Press, 1960).

QUATRAIN: "On a Photograph of My Grandfather" in *The Broken Frieze*, by Peter Everwine (Hillside Press, 1958); "I, the Childless One" in *Collected Poems*, by George Abbe (Richard R. Smith, 1961); "A Mad Negro Soldier Confined at Munich" in *Life Studies*, by Robert Lowell (Farrar, Straus & Cudahy, 1959); "The Lecturer Orders His Notes" in *The Walks Near Athens*, by Hollis Summers (Harper & Bros., 1959).

QUINTET: "The Black Swan" in *The Seven-League Crutches*, by Randall Jarrell (Harcourt, Brace & Co., 1951); "The Young Girl of the Mississippi Valley" in *Body of Waking*, by Muriel Rukeyser (Harper & Bros., 1958); "Seminary" in *The Middle Voice*, by Constance Carrier (Alan Swallow, 1955); "Poem Written in Late Autumn" by Albert Herzing in *Poets of Today VIII*, *op. cit.*

RANNAIGHEACHT GHAIRID: "Pocoangelini 3" by Lewis Turco in *Poetry*, Vol. 108, No. 3, July, 1966.

RIME ROYAL: "Beside My Grandmother" by Alfred M. Lee in *Midland*, ed. Engle (Random House, 1961): "Thoughts from the Boston Post Road" by Lewis Turco in *First Poems*, *op. cit.*

RISPETTO: "I Have No Praises" by David R. Slavitt in *Poets of Today VIII*, *op. cit.*; "Exeunt" in *Things of this World*, by Richard Wilbur (Harcourt, Brace & Co., 1956); "Blue Jay" by Robert Francis in *The Orb Weaver*, *op. cit.*; "Good Boy" by William Stafford in *A Houyhnhnm's Scrapbook*, no. 2, February, 1957; "The Voyage" in *Lupercal*, by Ted Hughes (Harper & Bros., 1960); "Although I Remember the Sound" by Robert Huff in *Colonel Johnson's Ride*, *op. cit.*

RONDEAU: "Death of a Vermont Farm Woman" by Barbara Howes in *Light and Dark*, *op. cit.*; "A Long Time Ago" by Nicholas Moore in *Poetry Quarterly* (England), Summer, 1950.

RONDEL: "Rondeau" by X. J. Kennedy in *Nude Descending*

a Staircase, op. cit.; "Rondel" in *Survivor's Leave* by Charles Causley, Aldington, Kent, England: Hand and Flower Press, 1953.

SAPPHICS: "Heart of Snow" by John Hollander in *A Crackling of Thorns, op. cit.*; "Legend for a Shield" in *Poems*, by Richmond Lattimore (University of Michigan Press, 1957); "Visitor" by Lewis Turco in *First Poems, op. cit.*; "Erinna to Sappho" by John Hollander in *A Crackling of Thorns, op. cit.*; "I Am Disquieted When I See Many Hills" in *Apples from Shinar*, by Hyam Plutzik (Wesleyan University Press, 1959).

SEPTET: "Here Come the Saints" in *Fighting Terms*, by Thom Gunn (Hawk's Well Press, 1958); "For a Friend Getting Married" in *Depth of Meaning*, by Christopher Wiseman (Iowa City: privately printed, 1960); "Lullaby" by James Scully in *Poetry* (Chicago), December, 1961; "Cages" in *Light in the West*, by Judson Jerome (Golden Quill Press, 1962).

SESTET: "April Inventory" in *Heart's Needle*, by W.D. Snodgrass (Alfred A. Knopf, Inc., 1959); "An End to No Encounter" by Norman Friedman in *Fine Arts Magazine* (University of Connecticut), Vol. III, no. 1, 1958; "Counting the Mad" in *The Summer Anniversaries*, by Donald Justice (Wesleyan University Press, 1960); "Autumnal Spring Song" by Vassar Miller in *New Orleans Poetry Journal*, Vol. I, no. 4, 1955.

SESTINA: "Sestina" in *On the Morning of Color*, by John Woods (Indiana University Press, 1961); "Sestina" in *The Aging Ghost*, by James Crenner (Golden Quill Press, 1964); "*Étude*: Andantino" in *Of the Festivity*, by William Dickey (Yale University Press, 1959); "A Dream Sestina" by Donald Justice in *The Summer Anniversaries, op. cit.*

SICILIAN OCTAVE: "The Widow's Rape" by Lewis Turco in *The Carolina Quarterly*, Vol. XVI, no. 1, 1963; "Daphne" by Fay Fox in *The Fenn Literary Omnibus*, Vol. I, 1963.

SKELTONICS: "Odds Bodkin's Strange Thrusts and Ravels" (a long satire on contemporary poetry) by Lewis Turco in

The Oberlin Quarterly, Part I: Vol. I, no. 1, 1963; Part II: Vol. I, no. 2, 1964.

SONNET: "Woman at the Window" in *The Wilderness and Other Poems* by Louis O. Coxe (University of Minnesota Press, 1958); "The Beautiful American Word, Sure" in *Summer Knowledge*, by Delmore Schwartz, (Doubleday & Co., Inc., 1959); "A Summer Idyll" in *The Self-Made Man*, by Reed Whittemore (The Macmillan Co., 1959); "Sonnet I" from "The Name of Love" in *Poems in Praise* by Paul Engle (Random House, 1959); "The City Considered as a Tulip Tree" in *The Man Behind You*, by Carl Bode (E. P. Dutton & Co., Inc., 1960); "Double Sonnet" in *A Summoning of Stones*, by Anthony Hecht (The Macmillan Co., 1954).

SPATIALS: "Mirror Image: Port-au-Prince" by Barbara Howes in *Light and Dark*, *op. cit.*; "Mirror," "Pendulum" in *The Carpentered Hen*, by John Updike (Harper & Bros., 1958); "400-Meter Free-Style" in *Halfway*, by Maxine W. Kumin (Holt, Rhineart, & Winston, 1961); "Totem" in *The Fortune Teller*, by John Holmes (Harper & Bros., 1961).

SPENSERIAN STANZA: "The Tandem Ride" in *Madonna of the Cello*, by Robert Bagg (Wesleyan University Press, 1961).

SPLIT COUPLET: "Two Octobers" by Richmond Lattimore in *Poems*, *op. cit.*; "Two Wrestlers" by Robert Francis in *The Orb Weaver*, *op. cit.*

STAVE: "Song for Strangers in Wales" in *Selected Poems* by John Malcolm Brinnin (Atlantic-Little, Brown, 1963).

TANKA: "After Masako" by Harriet Winnick in *Japan: Theme & Variations*, *op. cit.*

TERCET: "On the Calculus" by J. V. Cunningham in *The Exclusions of a Rhyme*, *op. cit.*; "Epitaph for Some Poet or Other" by Hayden Carruth in *The Crow and the Heart*, *op. cit.*; "Nutcracker" by John Updike in *The Carpentered Hen*, *op. cit.*

TERZA RIMA: "Home to Ostia" by G. F. Keithley in *The*

Wormwood Review, Vol. I, no. 2, 1960; "Admission of Guilt" in *Letter from a Distant Land,* by Philip Booth (Viking Press, 1957); "On a Certain Engagement South of Seoul" by Hayden Carruth in *The Crow and the Heart, op. cit.*; "Plato's Cave: The Annex" in *Mosaic,* by Frederic Will (Pennsylvania State University Press, 1959); "Meeting" in *The Hawk in the Rain,* by Ted Hughes (Harper & Bros., 1957).

TRIOLET: "Triolet" by Louise Townsend Nicholl in *The World's One Clock, op. cit.*; "Insight," "Wind-Song" in *Poems,* by Diane Musser (Theo. Gauss' Sons, Inc., 1958).

TRIPLET: "Harlowe Young" in *Aspects of Proteus,* by Hyam Plutzik (Harper & Bros., 1949); "Any Object" by May Swenson in *Poets of Today I,* ed. Wheelock (Chas. Scribner's Sons, 1954); "Scratch" from "The Wandering Jew" in *Works and Days,* by Irving Feldman (Atlantic-Little, Brown, 1961).

TRIVERSEN: "Words from England" in *Exiles and Marriages,* by Donald Hall (The Viking Press, 1955); "The Movement of the Worlds" by Kenneth McRobbie in *Poetry,* Vol. 96, no. 3, June, 1960; "Address" by Hayden Carruth in *The Crow and the Heart, op. cit.*; "Monday's Vision" in *Testament and Other Poems,* by John Fandel (Sheed & Ward, 1959); "Mulling It Over" by James Crenner in *The Aging Ghost, op. cit.*; "Six Sections of a Mask" by Lewis Turco in *First Poems, op. cit.*

VILLANELLE: "Do Not Go Gentle into That Good Night" by Dylan Thomas in *Collected Poems, op. cit.*; "Beyond Surprise" in *The Colours of Memory* by George Reavey (Grove Press, 1955); "Lament" by Sylvia Plath in *The New Orleans Poetry Journal,* Vol. I, no. 4, 1955; "Villanelle" by Weldon Kees in *Collected Poems, op. cit.*; "Women in Love" by Donald Justice in *The Summer Anniversaries, op. cit.*; "The Waking" by Theodore Roethke in *Words for the Wind, op. cit.*

Glossarial Index

abstract poem: verse that operates almost exclusively on the level of the *sonic pattern*. See also *nonsense verse*.

abstraction, 28

acatalexis, 23

accent, 15, 19

accented syllable, 16–17, 18–19, 21, 24

accentual forms, 44, 79, 89, 109, 130. See also *dipodics*.

accentual verse, 16, 18.

accentual-syllabic forms, 43, 46, 48–50, 53, 56, 58, 59, 63, 65, 71–72, 74, 79, 80–81, 82, 83, 84, 85, 86, 87, 88, 90, 91, 92, 97, 99, 105, 106–107, 108, 109, 111, 112, 116–118, 119, 120, 121, 123, 124, 128

accentual-syllabic verse, 3*ff*.

acephalexis, 23

acephalous, 23

acronym: a word made from the initials of words in a phrase or term.

ACROSTIC, 41

ADONIC, 108

AE FREISLIGHE, 42

aesthetic distance—see *objective*, *subjective*, *sensibility*, and *worth*.

ALBA, 80

ALCAICS, 43

ALEXANDRINE, 90, 120

allegory, 29

alliteration, 19, 25, 44, 130

alliterative sprung rhythm—see *sprung rhythm*.

allusion, 29–30

ambiguity, 30–31

American forms, 56, 69, 130

amphibrach, 15

amphimacer, 15

amphisbaenic rhyme, 25

ANACREONTICS, 80

anacrusis, 23

anagram: a word, phrase, or sentence made up of letters transposed from another word, phrase, or sentence. See RUNE.

analyzed rhyme, 24

anapest, 15

ANGLO-SAXON PROSODY, 44

anthology: a collection of literary pieces, usually by various authors.

antistrophe, 84

ANTITHETICAL PARALLELISM, 70

antonyms: words that have opposite meanings.

aphorism, 63

apocopated rhyme, 25

aposiopesis, 29

apostrophe, 29

approximate rhyme—see *off-rhyme.*

Arabic forms, 59, 106–107

archaism: a word or locution that is no longer to be found in normal contemporary speech; a linguistic anachronism.

archetype: seminal or original source; prototype.

architectonics—see *fusional level.*

argument—see *ideational level.*

arsis—see *unaccented syllable.*

association—see *connotation.*

assonance, 19–20, 25

AUBADE—see ALBA.

Augustan—see *neoclassical,* esp. entry 2.

AWDL GYWYDD, 45

BALLAD, 46, 131

BALLAD STANZA, 46

BALLADE, 47–48

BALLADE À DOUBLE REFRAIN, 48

BALLADE SUPRÊME, 47

bard, 18

baroque: an artistic and literary style of the seventeenth century characterized by fantastic and grotesque imagery and complexity of form.

beat—see *accent.*

beat poets: a school of poets that came to prominence in the 1950's. They were characterized by verse that was rhetorical and didactic. The content of their work was largely concerned with social criticism, and they used a variety of free-verse forms, but particularly the loose Biblical parallelisms of Whitman and the Imagist patterns of W.C. Williams and the early Ezra Pound.

bibliography of examples, 133–139

BLANK VERSE, 49

BOB—see BOB AND WHEEL.

BOB AND WHEEL, 50

breath pause, 69

BREF DOUBLE, 51

breve, 15

broken rhyme—see *apocopated rhyme*.

BUCOLIC—see ECLOGUE and PASTORAL.

burden, 26, 46

BURNS STANZA—see STANDARD HABBIE

BYR A THODDAID, 52

cacophony, 25

cadence—see *rhythm*.

caesura, 18, 20, 22, 44, 89

CALLIGRAMME—see SPATIALS.

Calliope—see *Muse*.

CANSO, 80

CANTICLE, 80

canto: a major sub-unit of a long poem; a verse chapter.

CANZO—see CANSO.

CANZONE—see CANSO.

carmen figuratum—see SPATIALS.

CAROL, 53

Caroline: the period of Charles I of England, 1625–49.

carpe diem motif: the "seize the day" convention of living the present moment to the fullest.

CASBAIRDNE, 54

catalexis, 23

CAUDATED SONNET, 117

cavalier poets: aristocratic poets of the *Caroline* period. See *Caroline*.

Celtic forms, 42; see also *Irish forms*, *Welsh forms*.

Chanson de Geste: a type of medieval French EPIC with marked lyric qualities.

CHANT, 80

CHANTEY, 80

CHANT ROYAL, 55

CHAUCERIAN STANZA—see RIME ROYAL.

CHORIAMBICS, 56

CINQUAIN, 56

classical: formal in structure, traditional in treatment; characteristic of Greek or Roman systems: objective rather than subjective, restrained rather than emotional. Clarity and simplicity of style are important features of classicism. Concerned with society, morals, manners, reason, common sense.

CLASSICAL HEXAMETER, 65

CLASSICAL PENTAMETER, 65

classical prosody—see *quantitative verse*.

CLERIHEW, 11

cliché: a trite expression.

diphthongs, 23, 66

dipodics: an accentual prosody standing halfway between Anglo-Saxon prosody and metrical verse. Many nursery rhymes are dipodic, as is much of the work of John Crowe Ransom and Theodore Roethke.

The dipodic line, like a hemistich of Anglo-Saxon prosody, contains two stresses; the first is a light (or secondary), stress, the second stress is heavy. However, in certain instances this pattern may be reversed. Normally, two dipodic lines form a half-unit, and two more lines are needed to complete the unit, which is rhymed; often the rhymes used are feminine:

> Óld Mother Goóse,
> When she wànted to wánder,
> Róde through the áir
> On a vèry fine gánder.

In effect, every two dipodic lines is a stich of Anglo-Saxon prosody divided by a caesura, and the four dipodic lines equal a couplet of rhymed Anglo-Saxon prosody (with or without alliteration):

> Óld Mother Goóse, · When she wànted to wánder,
> Róde through the áir · On a vèry fine gánder . . . ,

and sometimes the lines are written out in just such fashion:

> There wàs an old wóman · who lìved in a shóe.
> She had só many children · she dìdn't know whát to do.

For a related form, see *Skeltonics*. See also *sprung rhythm*.

dipody, 63

direct address—see *apostrophe*.

DIRGE—see ELEGY.

dispersion: a technique of e.e. cummings and others. A poem is first written in a traditional form. The poem's form is then disguised, or "dispersed," according to some pattern other than its original line or stanza structure, such as by phrase units, by halving the lines, by breaking lines at *caesuras*, or by running two or more lines together.

dissociation of sensibility—see *sensibility*.

dissonance, 25

distich—see *couplet*.

distributed stress: a situation that occurs when there is uncertainty concerning which of two consecutive syllables is to be accented. See *spondee*.

disyllabic: comprised of two syllables.

DITHYRAMB, 80

division, 15
DIZAIN, 48
DOGGEREL, 80, 109
DOUBLE ACROSTIC, 41
DOUBLE BALLADE, 47–48
DOUBLE BALLADE SUPRÊME, 47–48
double rhymes, 25, 42
DRAMATIC MONOLOGUE—see MONOLOGUE.
DRAMATICS, 63
dream vision: a convention wherein the poet falls asleep and has a
    dream, which he narrates.
DROIGHNEACH, 64
dúnadh, 42
ECLOGUE, 63, 81
Edwardians: a school of poets in England at the turn of the twentieth
    century.
eighteen-line forms, 37
eight-line forms, 36
ELEGIACS, 65
ELEGY, 80
eleven-line forms, 37
elision, 18, 22–23. See also *synalepha* and *syncope*.
ellipsis, 30
emblem, 29
embryonic rhyme—see *off-rhyme*.
ENCLOSED TERCET, 123
ENCLOSED TRIPLET, 128
encomiastic: written in praise of. See ODE.
end-stop, 22
end-words, 113–114.
English forms, 44, 50, 53, 74, 79, 80–81, 82, 84–85, 89, 105, 109,
    116–118, 120, 121
ENGLISH ODE, 84–85
ENGLISH SONNET, 116–117
ENGLYN CYRCH, 66
ENGLYN LLEDDFBROEST, 66
ENGLYN MILWR, 128
ENGLYN PENFYR, 128–129
ENGLYN PROEST DALGRON, 66
ENGLYN PROEST GADWYNOG, 67
ENGLYNS, 66–67, 128–129
ENGLYN UNODL CRWCA, 67
ENGLYN UNODL UNION, 67
enjambment, 18, 22

French forms, 47–48, 51, 53, 55, 75–79, 97, 100–104, 109, 113–114, 117, 125, 127, 131, 132

fusional level, 21

Georgians: a British school of poetry of the time of King George V of England.

GEORGICS, 63

GLOSE, 71

gnomic verse—see *aphorism*.

Gongorism: an affected style of writing similar to *euphuism*. After Luis de Góngora y Argote, Spanish poet, 1571–1627.

grammatics, 70

gratuitous metaphor—see *metaphoric construction*.

greater Ionic—see *Ionic*.

Greek forms, 43, 56, 65, 74, 80–81, 84

GWAWDODYN, 73

GWAWDODYN HIR, 73

GWAWDODYNS, 73

HAIKU, 123

half-rhyme—see *off-rhyme*.

hangers—see *outrides*.

head rhyme, 24

Hebrew prosody, 70

hemistich, 44, 89

HENDECASYLLABICS, 74

heptameter, 17

HEROIC COUPLET, 74

HEROIC LINE, 74

HEROIC OCTAVE, 99

HEROIC RISPETTO, 99

HEROICS, 74, 91, 99, 117

HEROIC SONNET, 117

HEROIC STANZA, 74, 91

HEROIC VERSE—see HEROICS.

hexameter, 17

hexasyllabic: comprised of six syllables.

HIEROGLYPHIC VERSE—see SPATIALS.

HIR A THODDAID, 75

HOKKU—see HAIKU.

hold—see *pause*.

homograph—see *homonyms*.

homonyms: words spelled alike, but having different meanings.

homophone—see *homonyms*.

HOMOSTROPHIC ODE, 84

mythopoesis: myth-making.

mythopoet: a poet who in his work practices *mythopoeia*.

narrative, 46, 131

narrative forms—see VERSE NARRATIVES.

NASHERS, 69

near-rhyme—see *off-rhyme*.

neoclassical: 1) contemporary or modern, but having the qualities associated with classical poetry; 2) English poetry of the eighteenth century: *Augustan*.

neologism: a coined or newly invented word.

nine-line forms, 36

nineteen-line forms, 38

ninety-eight-line forms, 38

nonasyllabic: comprised of nine syllables.

nonsense verse, 79, 80, 109

normative meter, 17–18

numbers—see *meter* and *metrics*.

NURSERY RHYME, 80

objective: without emotional involvement; dispassionate, analytical.

objective correlative—see *concretion* and *sensory pattern*.

oblique rhyme—see *off-rhyme*.

occasional poetry: verse composed in commemoration. See particularly the ODE and the ELEGY.

OCTAVE, 83

octave forms, 36

octosyllabic: comprised of eight syllables.

ODE, 80, 84–85

off-rhyme, 19, 25

OMAR STANZA—see RUBAI.

one-line forms, 32–33

onomatopoeia, 29

open couplet—see *enjambment*.

orchestration, 28, 30

organic metaphor—see *metaphoric construction*.

OTTAVA RIMA, 86

outrides—Gerard Manley Hopkins's term for the unaccented syllables in accentual verse.

oxymoron, 28

paeon: any one of four metrical feet; each is composed of four syllables one stressed and three unstressed: $-$ʋʋʋ, ʋ$-$ʋʋ, ʋʋ$-$ʋ, ʋʋʋ$-$.

palindrome: any language unit that reads the same backward or forward.

PALINODE, 87

paranomasia—see *pun*.

paraphones—see *off-rhyme.*

pararhyme—see *off-rhyme.*

Parnassian poetry: poetry of a second order written by poets of a first order.

Parnassian poets: a mid-nineteenth-century school of French poetry.

Parnassus: the mountain sacred to Apollo and the Muses, symbolic of poetry in particular and the arts in general.

parody: caricature of a well-known literary work. A satiric mode.

PASTORAL, 80–81

PASTORAL ELEGY, 81

pathetic fallacy: as distinguished from *personification,* which is a form of metaphor, pathetic fallacy is the endowment of inanimate or subhuman objects with absurdly human characteristics, i.e., "The little white cloud that cried."

pattern, 21; see also *forms.*

patterned verse—see SPATIALS.

pause—see *caesura, end-stop,* and *phrasing.*

PEARLINE STANZA, 89

Pegasus: a winged horse of Greek mythology. With a blow of his hoof he caused Hippocrene, the fountain of poetic inspiration, to spring from Mount Helicon; symbolic of poetic inspiration.

pentasyllabic: comprised of five syllables.

periphrasis, 30

personification, 29

PETRARCHAN SONNET—see ITALIAN SONNET.

phanopoeia—see *image, sensory pattern.*

phrasing, 22, 69–70, 130. See also *projective verse* and *variable foot.*

PINDARIC ODE, 84

poem: an artifice of language. See *poet.* See also p. 21.

poem forms, 41, 46, 47–48, 51, 53, 55, 56, 63, 69–70, 71, 74, 75, 76–78, 79, 80–81, 82, 84–85, 87, 88, 91, 92, 99, 100–102, 103, 104, 105, 106–107, 108, 109, 111, 112, 113–114, 116–118, 119, 121, 122, 123, 125, 127, 130, 131, 132

poesy; poetry—see *poem.*

poet: an artificer of language, as distinguished from the fictionist, who is an artificer of written narrative; the dramatist, who is an artificer of theatrical narrative; and the essayist, who is an artificer of rhetorical exposition. The poet is a writer whose focus is primarily on the language itself; the fictionist and dramatist concentrate upon the story-line, the essayist concentrates upon the examination of a subject. Thus, poetry is not determined by a particular mode, such as verse, for even prose may be utilized to concentrate upon language (see FREE VERSE).

The distinction, then, is not between poetry and prose, but between poetry and fiction; poetry and drama; poetry and essay. Thus, fiction may be written in verse and still be fiction, not poetry (if the concentration is upon the story-line rather than upon the language); plays may be written in verse, and essays in verse, and still be plays or essays. See also *bard* and *maker*.

poetaster: an unskilled dabbler in versification.

poetic: partaking of the qualities associated with poetry.

poetic diction: as opposed to intensified normal speech, poetic diction is contrived of speech forms invented for the purpose of verse composition.

poetic justice: punishment, administered by the gods (evidently with the counsel of the Muses), to fit the crime.

poetic license: a document issued by the Anti-Muses to poetasters. Allegedly, this license gives its holder the right to do anything he pleases in verse, and to call the results poetry; however, the poetic license owns many of the characteristics of Confederate Money.

poetics—see *prosody*.

poet laureate: 1) an academic degree; 2) an official title.

poetry—see *poem*, *poet*. Any writing which successfully focuses on language.

Polyhymnia—see *Muse*.

polyphonic prose, 69

Portuguese forms, 71–72

POULTER'S MEASURE, 90

primary accent—see *ictus*.

PRIMER COUPLET, 63

projective verse: essentially, a prosody based partly upon a system of variable accentuals (see *variable foot*), and partly upon a system of grammatics. See *breath pause*, *parallelism*, *phrasing*, TRIVERSEN, *verse paragraph*, *verse sentence*.

PROSE POEM, 69

prosodic symbols, 15–20

prosodic systems—see *prosody*.

prosody, 15–20, 68–70

prosopopoeia—see *personification*.

PROTHALAMION, 80

pun, 27

pure poetry: poetry written simply on the level of *euphony* and without any larger intention to instruct, moralize, or edify.

pyrrhic, 15

QASĪDA, 59

quality, 18, 21

quantitative verse, 15

quantity, 18, 21

sprung rhythm: Gerard Manley Hopkins's term for the accentual rhythms that are to be found in *Anglo-Saxon prosody*, *dipodics*, and *Skeltonics*. The difference is that the term "sprung rhythm" is descriptive of the general accentual prosody that includes all three forms.

Anglo-Saxon prosody, dipodics, and Skeltonics utilize accents that are made all the heavier by means of alliteration or substitution. The first case is explained in the sections dealing with the three forms named, and in the chapter on *Metrics*.

In the case of *substitution*, Hopkins points out that sprung rhythm arises when a reverse foot is substituted for a foot of the running rhythm (or *normative meter*) of a poem (i.e., a dactyl for an iamb in an iambic poem). He distinguishes between the "alliterative" sprung rhythm and the "substitutive" sprung rhythm by pointing out that the latter is *counterpoint:* ". . . the super-inducing or *mounting* of a new rhythm upon the old [normative]; and since the new or mounted rhythm is actually heard and at the same time the mind naturally supplies the [normative] rhythm . . . , two rhythms are. . . running at once and we have something answerable to counterpoint in music." This same point is made in simpler language in the chapter on *Metrics* and elsewhere in *The Book of Forms*. For Hopkins's detailed theory one may consult the "Author's Preface" to the *Poems* (1876–1889).

In a poem written in sprung rhythm, other than in the three forms named, the number of accents of each line is determined by the author.

An accentual system that is not a part of the sprung-rhythm theory is the American *variable foot* prosody of William Carlos Williams. Williams's invention is not dependent upon alliteration or substitution.

variable syllabics: the prosody of Marianne Moore and others. The lines of a single stanza of poetry may vary in length; i.e., in a five-line stanza the syllabic lengths of lines may be three, five, seven, four, and two syllables respectively. Succeeding stanzas will normally retain the same counts as the first stanza, line for line.

variable syllable: a syllable that may or may not be accented, depending on its position in the context of the poem. See also *distributed stress*.

vehicle—see *metaphoric construction*.

verbal texture—see *sonics, cynghanedd*.

vers de société: light verse concerned with manners and customs.

verse, 68, 70. See also *line of verse* and *stich*.

verse chapter—see *canto* and *fit*.

verse foot, 15

VERSE NARRATIVES, 131

verse paragraph, 69

verse sentence, 130

vers libre—see *free verse*.

Victorian poets: romantic poets of the second half of the nineteenth century.

vignette, 131

VILLANELLE, 132

VIRELAI, 77–78

virgule, 15

visible level, 21

vocalic assonance—see *assonance*.

vowels, 22–23, 44

Welsh forms, 45, 52, 57, 59, 60–62, 66–67, 73, 75, 95–96, 126, 128–129

w-glide, 22

WHEEL—see BOB AND WHEEL.

worth: a value judgment concerning the intent of a poem, and the achievement of that intent by the poet. It has been said that a poem may be worthy in one of three general ways: 1) by reason of its saying something completely new; 2) by reason of its offering a new insight or perspective on an already established idea or subject; 3) by reason of its couching an established idea or subject in a new and interesting style. See *tact, sensibility*.

wrenched accent: when, in context, the metric of the line demands that a normally unaccented syllable take a stress, the result will be wrenched accent.

wrenched rhyme, 24

word-count prosody, 70

y-glide, 22